The Vocabulary Builder

Other Books by Judi Kesselman-Turkel and Franklynn Peterson

BOOKS IN THIS SERIES
The Grammar Crammer: How to Write Perfect Sentences
Note-Taking Made Easy
Research Shortcuts
Secrets to Writing Great Papers
Study Smarts: How to Learn More in Less Time
Test-Taking Strategies

OTHER COAUTHORED BOOKS FOR ADULTS
The Author's Handbook
The Do-It-Yourself Custom Van Book (with Dr. Frank Konishi)
Eat Anything Exercise Diet (with Dr. Frank Konishi)
Good Writing
Homeowner's Book of Lists
The Magazine Writer's Handbook

COAUTHORED BOOKS FOR CHILDREN
I Can Use Tools
Vans

BY JUDI KESSELMAN-TURKEL
Stopping Out: A Guide to Leaving College and Getting Back In

BY FRANKLYNN PETERSON
The Build-It-Yourself Furniture Catalog
Children's Toys You Can Build Yourself
Freedom from Fibromyalgia (with Nancy Selfridge, M. D.)
Handbook of Lawn Mower Repair
Handbook of Snowmobile Maintenance and Repair
How to Fix Damn Near Everything
How to Improve Damn Near Everything around Your Home

The Vocabulary Builder

The Practically Painless Way to a Larger Vocabulary

Judi Kesselman-Turkel and Franklynn Peterson

THE UNIVERSITY OF WISCONSIN PRESS

The University of Wisconsin Press
1930 Monroe Street
Madison, Wisconsin 53711

www.wisc.edu/wisconsinpress/

3 Henrietta Street
London WC2E 8LU, England

Library of Congress Cataloging-in-Publication Data
Kesselman-Turkel, Judi.
The vocabulary builder : the practically painless way to a larger
vocabulary /
    Judi Kesselman-Turkel and Franklynn Peterson.
    p. cm.
    Originally published: Chicago : Contemporary Books, c1982.
    ISBN 0-299-19204-0 (pbk. : alk. paper)
    1. Vocabulary. 2. Word games. 3. Puzzles. I Peterson,
Franklynn. II. Title.
PE1449.K37   2003
428.1—dc21   2003050149

To Fran, who loves to do puzzles

CONTENTS

The Vocabulary Builder

INTRODUCTION
(Some Up-Front Words from the Authors)

We believe that vocabulary-building should be fun and easy. That's why we created this little book of word games. We also believe that only useful words are worth learning to use. So instead of choosing words to fit a format or selecting them at random from a dictionary, as some other vocabulary-building books do, we've taken real words from the pages of current magazines that are found in high school and college classrooms and libraries. Then each word appears approximately four times through the book, often in slightly different context or form, so you can learn a word's several synonyms and definitions, not just one of its uses.

The 600+ words we've chosen are alphabetized at the end in a mini-dictionary whose definitions are as simple and clear as we can make them. The definitions aren't all-inclusive, and in some cases they would be more precise if we used words that are themselves uncommon and difficult to understand. When we had to decide between clarity and precision, we opted for clarity.

For the person with average vocabulary, the best way to begin using the book is to scan the back-of-the-book dictionary whenever an answer is elusive. Each time you look up a word, its meaning is reinforced. By the second or third time you meet a difficult word, it should no longer be a stranger. By the time you're halfway through these games—even if you prefer to skip around rather than play them in order—you should be able to do well without consulting the dictionary.

The individual who prefers challenge, or whose vocabulary is well above average, should consult the dictionary entries only for words he misses.

We hope you enjoy these games as much as we enjoyed inventing them. If you do, tell your friends—and our publisher—and we'll get to work on another volume of stumpers.

Judi Kesselman-Turkel
Franklynn Peterson

1. FOR STARTERS

For starters, here are some common *prefixes,* or word starters. They begin the words that are defined below. If you remember the meaning of a prefix, you can often use it as a clue to a word that has slipped your tongue. (For added clues, we supply *Words to choose from.*)

Prefix	Meaning	English word's meaning	Word?
dis	not	(1) to claim no responsibility for	_____
		(2) to make someone not calm	_____
e, es, ex	out, out of,	(3) out of sight, obscured	_____
		(4) to figure out	_____
	from	(5) to bring out	_____
		(6) turning the mind from reality	_____
		(7) from official authority	_____
de	off, away,	(8) to turn away, keep from acting	_____
		(9) the product of wearing away	_____
im, in	not	(10) show of no concern	_____
		(11) not careful in actions	_____
im, in	on, in	(12) to force on people	_____
per	through	(13) to spread throughout	_____
		(14) to become aware of through the senses	_____
pre	before	(15) something needed beforehand	_____
		(16) to know before it happens	_____

		(17) to prevent by prior action	_____
retro	back	(18) a look back at past works	_____
re	back, again	(19) to put back in former condition	_____
		(20) to say over and over again	_____

Words to choose from: deter, ex cathedra, disavow, disconcert, insouciance, perceive, presage, reiterate, indiscreet, detritus, educe, eclipsed, reconstitute, preclude, impose, pervade, escapism, retrospective, elicit, prerequisite.

2. IT'S ALL IN HOW

We all know the expression "It's all in how you look at things." Below are 20 different ways of looking at things. How many are you familiar with?

1. Reagan's advisors were sufficiently *chagrined* about poverty to seek some remedy to unemployment.
   (a) chastened (b) charged up (c) embarrassed (d) sorry

2. To diffuse criticism, the Senator mixed *candor and contrition.*
   (a) truth and apology (b) suggestion and sorrow
   (c) innocence and triteness (d) cunning and contrivance

3. The posters reflect the *animosity* between the two groups.
   (a) hatred (b) war (c) animal behavior (d) love

4. The Premier gave a *conciliatory* speech in which he stated, "We are not seeking confrontation."
   (a) advisory (b) conversational (c) demanding (d) friendly

5. He made some *desultory* remarks about the state of the nation.
   (a) off the topic (b) unsolicited (c) sour (d) thoughtless

6. The speaker displayed a *disconcerting* lode of misinformation and a *dubious* grasp of details.
   (a) unconnected, careless (b) distracting, doubtful
   (c) bewildering, questionable (d) large, twofold

7. The President was criticized last week for his *fecklessness* on foreign policy.
   (a) recklessness (b) ineffectiveness (c) fickleness
   (d) dirty tricks

8. The general has grown more *hawkish* toward his enemies since retirement.
   (a) graceful (b) flighty (c) liberal (d) saber-rattling

9. When it comes to clothes, she's an *individualist.*
   (a) knee-jerk liberal (b) independent thinker
   (c) capitalist (d) eccentric

10. The loss of the game was blamed on her *intransigence.*
    (a) rigid sense of values (b) obstinacy
    (c) failure to show up (d) entrance

11. The instructor's remarks are occasionally *irreverent.*
    (a) beside the point (b) ghost written (c) pious (d) flippant

12. They plan to challenge the *obstructionist* legislators at the polls.
    (a) obstinate (b) standing in the way (c) structured
    (d) walleyed

13. With total irony, they cautioned the old man not to let his *penury* spoil his retirement plans.
    (a) poverty (b) writings (c) frugality (d) spendthriftness

14. The "hawks" seemed to derive a certain *relish* from the Arab-Israeli unrest.
    (a) dessert (b) extra something (c) pleasure (d) sense of reality

15. A murderer's *infamy* usually increases in proportion to the *renown* of the victim.
    (a) bad reputation, fame (b) evil deed, smartness
    (c) bad intention, refusal (d) horror, fight

16. I'm unable to *speculate* on what may have gone wrong.
    (a) see (b) think (c) theorize (d) decide

17. The claim is nonsense, but he made skillful use of the data to get his *spurious* message across.
    (a) speedy (b) phony (c) digging (d) sputtering

18. This book was not produced by a *stolid* publishing house.
    (a) stately (b) well-entrenched (c) unimaginative (d) old

19. We've got the most *stringent* gun control statutes in the United States.
    (a) strict (b) strident (c) strong (d) pungent

20. We need to back up our threats with *telling* action.
    (a) ordered (b) effective (c) resounding (d) tenacious

3. MYSTERY ISTORY

Each of the words in the left-hand column includes the letters *is*. But that's all tney have in common. In the right-hand column are clues to the words' definitions. Figure out which word goes with which clue.

1. activist		a.	principled draft dodger
2. anguish		b.	can't add, can't subtract
3. boisterous		c.	risky, but the goal is worth it
4. burnish		d.	help get the word out
5. bristle		e.	if looks could kill
6. disciple		f.	the people, right or wrong
7. enterprise		g.	the lovebirds broke up
8. fiscal		h.	what a rowdy gang
9. miscalculation		i.	felt it clear to the gut
10. pacifist		j.	it's more complicated than that
11. populist		k.	in such torment, he tears his hair
12. relish		l.	ask for it in writing
13. requisition		m.	that cause is worth fighting for
14. schism		n.	it's so good I can taste it
15. simplistic		o.	rub it so it shines
16. visceral		p.	where there's money there's taxes

4. ALPHABET SOUP CROSSWORD

To help you with this puzzle, we'll give the first letter of each word you must find.

Across

1. A   for reducing or ending
3. H   for a bunch of unrelated things
12. D   for making impure
15. F   for much noise by many people
16. C   for caution
19. M   for a big one
23. G   for wearing
26. S   for an orderly system
29. O   for accommodating
30. P   for rows
31. F   for a celebration
32. L   for lack of tight control
33. A   for having cut back

Down

2. B   for someone who was awarded money
4. D   for part of, because of
5. P   for a tricky tactic
6. O   for too much fun in too little time
7. Q   for energy
8. C   for influence
9. P   plus eate for spreading throughout
10. J   for government
11. O   for something bad may happen
13. E   for something proved experimentally
14. U   for a brat
17. S   for a sudden burst
18. I   for lacking in power
20. T   for a triumvirate
21. K   for a noisemaker
22. N   for helping develop
24. Z   for fanatical devotion
25. W   for doing something
27. T   for slanted
28. V   for rival

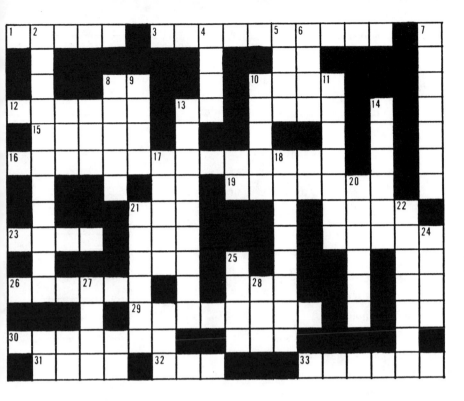

5. END PLAY #1

Let's focus on the word ending *ly*, which is often added to an adjective to make an adverb. Sometimes only the word changes; the meaning remains pretty much the same. Sometimes, however, the meaning changes slightly, too. Supply each missing *ly* adverb from the definition of the *adjective* it comes from—and then circle the adverbs that changed meaning when *ly* was added. (As an additional clue, we give the first letter of each word. For more help, scan the Mini-Dictionary.)

1. eager   a _____

2. not appeasable   i _____

3. tending to keep one from using something   p _____

4. skillful   d _____

5. not fit or proper   u _____

6. so-called   a _____

7. urgent   i _____

8. crooked, indirect, or underhanded   o _____

9. painful or tender   s _____

10. open to view; plausible   o _____

11. guiltless; morally right   r _____

12. last, farthest, most basic, or most extreme   u _____

13. friendly and unreserved   a _____

14. obstinate or cranky   p _____

15. horrifying, disgusting   a _____

16. not showing good judgment   i _____

17. awe-inspiring   f _____

18. permanent   i _____

19. independent, self-contained   a _____

20. guilty, blameworthy   c _____

6. HOW VERBAL ARE YOU #1

There's a verb in the language to describe every conceivable shade of action. Are you facile enough with your verbs to express all the following actions?

1. to remind about duties or obligations *(8 letters beginning with a)*

2. to absorb into the group or culture *(10 letters beginning with a)*

3. to raise someone's spirits *(6 letters beginning with b)*

4. to halt an action or event that has just gotten underway *(5 letters beginning with a)*

5. to question in order to obtain useful information *(7 letters beginning with d)*

6. to distract attention from a distressing situation *(6 letters beginning with d)*

7. to lower a person's status *(6 letters beginning with d)*

8. to take over a situation or group *(5 letters beginning with c)*

9. to check or control *(4 letters beginning with c)*

10. to plan out skillfully *(8 letters beginning with e)*

11. to prohibit the transportation of freight *(7 letters beginning with e)*

12. to call to mind *(5 letters beginning with e)*

13. to lessen in intensity *(5 letters beginning with a)*

14. to join into a systematic whole *(10 letters beginning with a)*

15. to open a subject for discussion *(6 letters beginning with b)*

16. to obscure or darken *(7 letters beginning with e)*

17. to spread out strategically *(6 letters beginning with d)*

18. to sway from side to side *(6 letters beginning with c)*

19. to give promise of future action or performance *(5 letters beginning with a)*

20. to make physically or emotionally impure *(6 letters beginning with d)*

Words to choose from: abate, abort, admonish, articulate, assimilate, augur, broach, buoy up, careen, co-opt, curb, debrief, defile, demean, deploy, divert, eclipse, embargo, engineer, evoke.

7. FIRST SPOTLIGHT

Throughout this book we'll spotlight some words that have interesting histories. The first comes from the novel *Candide* by Voltaire, in which there was a character who believed that this was the best of all possible worlds and that everything that happened in it eventually turned out for the best. The name of that character has come down to us as an adjective which is used even today to describe someone who sees the bright side of every misfortune. That word is spelled out in the first letter of every word defined below. How soon can you fill in all its letters and use them to help you find the rest of the defined words?

1. unreal (*6 letters*) _____
2. unprepared words (*2 words*) _____
3. to sting (*6 letters*) _____
4. taunt (*4 letters*) _____
5. in transition (*5 letters*) _____
6. throw out (*4 letters*) _____
7. know-how (*5 letters*) _____
8. barnstorm (*5 letters*) _____
9. time between (*7 letters*) _____
10. mark of praise (*8 letters*) _____
11. ineffective remedy (*7 letters*) _____

8. DISTANT RELATIVES

Each column contains 18 sets of words whose meanings are distantly related. The right-hand column contains the synonyms for the words in the left-hand column. First select the set of words from the right-hand column that goes with each left-hand set. Then tell which word in the set matches which synonym. Write your answers in the spaces below.

1. (a) outdoing,   A. (1) lustrous, (2) burnished
   (b) dominating
2. (a) period after,   B (1) cuckold,
   (b) reaction   (2) contretemps
3. (a) enthusiast, (b) agitator   C. (1) capping,
                                 (2) overarching
4. (a) deep pit, (b) penetrate   D. (1) sway, (2) regime
   deeply
5. (a) obedient, (b) friendly   E. (1) fomenter, (2) activist
6. (a) mysterious, (b) secret   F. (1) relevant, (2) context
7. (a) mortified spouse,   G. (1) backlash, (2) aftermath
   (b) embarrassing occasion
8. (a) motivating,   H. (1) affable, (2) compliant
   (b) stimulating

9. (a) shining, (b) shined
10. (a) surrounding, (b) belonging
11. (a) consciousness, (b) alertness
12. (a) authority, (b) government
13. (a) damaged, (b) destroyed
14. (a) generalization, (b) comparison
15. (a) troubles, (b) to trouble
16. (a) contrary, (b) to contradict
17. (a) misfit, (b) mistake
18. (a) uninteresting, (b) uninterested

I. (1) galvanizing, (2) causal
J. (1) beset, (2) adversity
K. (1) abyss, (2) fathom
L. (1) arcane, (2) laconic
M. (1) anomaly, (2) miscalculation
N. (1) strangulated, (2) impaired
O. (1) tedious, (2) perfunctory
P. (1) acuity, (2) sentience
Q. (1) belie, (2) perverse
R. (1) analogy, (2) abstraction

Answers

1:___, a-___, b-___.   7:___, a-___, b-___.   13:___, a-___, b-___.
2:___, a-___, b-___.   8:___, a-___, b-___.   14:___, a-___, b-___.
3:___, a-___, b-___.   9:___, a-___, b-___.   15:___, a-___, b-___.
4:___, a-___, b-___.   10:___, a-___, b-___.   16:___, a-___, b-___.
5:___, a-___, b-___.   11:___, a-___, b-___.   17:___, a-___, b-___.
6:___, a-___, b-___.   12:___, a-___, b-___.   18:___, a-___, b-___.

9. SCRAMBLED MAXIMS #1

A maxim is a general truth, usually stated in simple and picturesque words. If you fill in the correct word for each definition, the first letter of each word, read in sequence, spells out the first and last halves of two maxims. Elsewhere among our *Scrambled Maxims* you'll find the other halves of the two maxims. (To start you off, we've filled in two definitions. And we've included *Words to choose from* for the easily discouraged.)

1. early   _____

2. imprecise representation   _____

3. suicidal   _____

4. living things' relation to the environment   _____

5. malarkey   _____

6. bottomless gulf   _____

7. positive statement   <u>yes</u>_____

8. relinquish voluntarily   _____

9. strong longing   _____

10. worsen physically   _____

11. relax   _____

12. completely clear   _____

13. having to do with the study of religion   _____

14. the campaign trail   _____

15. earthquake center   _____

16. agree to   _____

17. mixture of various things   _____

18. capable of being given an approximate value   _____

19. consolation   _____

20. to cause agony   _____

21. pale   _____

22. to cause constant suffering   _____

23. exclamation when puzzle is completed   <u>yay</u>_____

Words to choose from: comply, theological, afflict, agonize, wan, solace, hustings, hokum, abstraction, amalgam, abyss, waive, kamikaze, matinal, impair, ecology, laze, explicit, hankering, tangible, epicenter.

10. ODS AND ENDS

Each word defined below has *od, and,* or *end* in it. How many words can you fill in?

1. a sedative   _____
2. patronize   _____
3. make-believe crying   _____
4. fiery   _____
5. soothing   _____
6. feud   _____
7. wander   _____
8. platform   _____
9. forewarn   _____
10. magnificent   _____
11. to station   _____
12. foolishness   _____
13. sincerity   _____
14. meeting place   _____
15. insinuation   _____
16. foolish   _____
17. central states   _____
18. strategy   _____
19. surpass   _____
20. unfashionable   _____
21. mediate   _____
22. outpost   _____
23. copy   _____
24. jumble   _____
25. caricature   _____

Words to choose from: anodyne, bland, candor, condescend, crocodile tears, doddering, fandango, grandiose, heartland, hinterland, hodgepodge, incendiary, innuendo, lodge, meander, methodology, moderate, outmoded, parody, podium, portend, rendering, rendezvous, transcend, vendetta.

11. MEET THE PRESS #1

All these sentences come straight from one news article in the popular press. Would you have trouble reading it? Circle the closest synonym for the italicized word or words in each sentence.

1. From the halls of Congress to the *posh* living rooms of Beverly Hills, Americans are becoming aware of the nuclear threat.
   (a) partying (b) comfortable (c) chic (d) gaudy

2. The new movement includes doctors and lawyers with *impeccable* establishment credentials.
   (a) unused (b) faultless (c) faulty (d) guilty

3. The resolution called upon the President to invite the Soviets to negotiate on the *proliferation* of nuclear technology.
   (a) rapid growth (b) airlift (c) creation (d) prohibition

4. The book's theme is an impassioned argument that nuclear weapons have made war *obsolete* and world government *imperative.*
   (a) unfashionable, unquestionable (b) out of date, urgent
   (c) unnecessary, important (d) repulsive, silly

5. They're rushing into print a paperback *primer* on the subject.
   (a) volume (b) first-aid (c) pumper (d) textbook

6. The exchange between Reagan and Brezhnev probably did more to *augment* superpower tensions than to ease them.
   (a) predict (b) rend (c) heighten (d) lessen

7. Brezhnev declared that the Soviet Union would *unilaterally* dismantle some of its missiles this year.
   (a) on its own (b) by agreement (c) later (d) once

8. Reagan said that wouldn't necessarily put him in an *analogous* position.
   (a) similar (b) analyzing (c) logical (d) awkward

9. It might compel Brezhnev to take *retaliatory* steps.
   (a) related (b) tailor-made (c) revenging (d) retail

10. It's that kind of scare talk that is *galvanizing* the nuclear-disarmament advocates.
    (a) coating (b) leading (c) frightening (d) arousing

11. "To have great appeal," she said, "her plan must be simple, effective, and *bilateral.*"
    (a) two-faced (b) accounting for both sides (c) easily digested
    (d) not made too late

12. Two organizations *exemplify* the passions and concerns of the nuclear freeze movement: Ground Zero and PSR.
    (a) leave behind (b) amplify (c) typify (d) hate

13. They're planning a *catalytic* launching of a mass effort to make the nation discuss the threat of nuclear war.
    (a) catastrophic (b) cataclysmic (c) rousing (d) dousing

14. He said, "The ball is rolling and we want to give it *momentum.*"
    (a) a push (b) strength (c) time (d) a reason

15. PSR was until recently a *moribund* organization devoted to detailing the medical consequences of nuclear war.
    (a) dying (b) glum (c) hidebound (d) shameful

16. Its *credibility* was achieved as a single-issue organization.
    (a) acceptance (b) reputation (c) believability (d) credentials

17. In an ongoing series of *symposia* across the country, members lecture about the Bomb.
    (a) formal discussions (b) informal get-togethers (c) concerts (d) gyms

18. The U.S. and the Soviet Union already have large enough arsenals to *annihilate* each other many times over.
    (a) sweep the floor with (b) mop up (c) chew up (d) wipe out

19. Some critics charge that the movement is *ultimately* a *pacifist* one.
    (a) largely, watery (b) in the end, appeasing (c) at last, thumb-sucking (d) lately, prissy

20. The movement is still rather *amorphous* and unorganized.
    (a) ambivalent (b) sleepy (c) dead (d) formless

12. WORD TWINS

Many words have twins that mean exactly, or almost exactly, the same thing. There are a number of twins in our vocabulary list. Let's focus on some of them. (If you'd like help, scan the Mini-Dictionary.)

1. Two words that both mean quarrelsome   b _____
                                                                b _____

2. Two words that both mean caustic   a _____
                                                                    m _____

3. Two words that both mean counterfeit   b _____

4. The first word means esteem, the second a mark of esteem, the third to show esteem
    a _____
    a _____
    l _____

5. To relieve or reduce anything
    a _____
   To relieve or reduce pain
    a _____

6. Exuberantly loud
    b _____
   Offensively loud
    r _____
   Offensively loud or conspicuous
    b _____

7. Friendly to gain favor
    i _____
   Friendly and forgiving
    c _____

8. Three words that mean bring out
    e _____
    e _____
    e _____

9. To shift back and forth
    f _____
   To turn round and round
    g _____

10. Two little verbs of ridicule
    g _____
    j _____

11. When peace will reign on Earth
    m _____
   When persons will ascend to heaven
    a _____

12. The first is an all-out attack, the second a small raid
    o _____
    f _____

13. Idle chatter between friends
    p _____
   Idle chatter between nations
    p _____

14. Two words that both mean outdated
    o _____
    o _____

15. Two words that mean hard to pin down
    e _____
    e _____

16. Two words that show denial: the first a noun, the second a verb
    d _____
    d _____

17. Two words that both mean obstinate or ill-tempered
    p _____
    p _____

18. Two words that both mean supposed
    a _____
    p _____

19. The first is to cause emotional harm, the second to distress acutely, the third the resulting distress
    t _____
    a _____
    a _____

20. Action on behalf of one side of an issue
    u _____
   Acting strongly to support one side of an issue
    a _____

13. HOW DOES IT LOOK?

One word can often take the place of many—if you know the word.

1. That building is _____. *(disproportionately low and thick)*
2. He has a _____ complexion. *(pale and sickly)*
3. He walks with a _____ skip. *(young and fresh as spring)*
4. She favored us with a _____ smile. *(here just for the moment)*
5. His hat was _____. *(slanted to one side)*
6. Her chin is quite _____. *(sticking out)*
7. The car was _____-___. *(increased in power)*
8. The clouds _____ across the sky. *(were blown by the wind)*
9. The walls were painted _____. *(a muddy red-yellow color)*
10. The St. Bernard was _____ in size. *(as big as an elephant)*
11. Vincent Price often looked _____ in his films. *(as gruesome as a dead thing)*
12. There are _____ flowers in the field. *(an uncountable number)*
13. The President's guards were dressed in _____. *(civilian clothes)*
14. The suit is _____. *(dull brown)*
15. Both husband and wife are _____. *(big and fat)*
16. He walks with a _____ gait. *(looking old and feeble)*
17. He is a _____ young man. *(unlively and unemotional)*
18. The car gleams as if it were _____. *(rubbed to shininess)*
19. The ghost I saw was _____. *(had no definite shape)*
20. He _____ when he speaks. *(stutters and stumbles)*

Words to choose from: bumbles, burnished, doddering, drab, myriad, mammoth, scudded, prominent, transient, vernal, squat, wan, skewed, souped-up, ocher, macabre, mufti, gross, bland, amorphous.

14. IT'S PERSONAL

Name the one word that sums up each of the people described below.

1. a trusted advisor
2. the person who had your job before you
3. a war resister
4. a big shot
5. a servant or lowly worker
6. a representative to another country
7. a person who's hard to figure out
8. an exile
9. someone from outer space
10. an inexperienced person
11. a believer in literally following the Bible's teachings
12. the head of a business
13. someone who attempts to avoid reality
14. a person left money in a will
15. someone who helps spread another's ideas
16. the purchaser of valuable artwork
17. one who is a perfect example for others
18. one who tries out for a job
19. someone who is a hundred years old
20. someone who's been abandoned by society
21. a person who disagrees with majority opinion
22. your opponent in a battle or contest
23. a god in human form
24. someone who causes others to change without any change in herself
25. an expert attached to a diplomatic embassy
26. one of the fighters
27. a man whose wife is unfaithful
28. a fanatic

29. someone whose career is being sponsored

30. a youngster who lives in the streets

Words to choose from: ecclesiastic, mentor, urchin, adversary, catalyst, fundamentalist, predecessor, pacifist, mogul, apotheosis, enigma, extraterrestrial, beneficiary, belligerent, protégé, centenarian, aspirant, menial,

15. SECOND SPOTLIGHT

Let's turn the spotlight on another word with an interesting history. This one comes from a novel by Rabelais and was originally the name of a gigantic king who had a great capacity for food and drink. The name was more recently given to an ape in an American film. We use it today as an·adjective to describe a common attribute of the ape and the king. The word is spelled out in the first letter of every word defined below. Fill in the spotlight word, and use it to find the rest of the defined words.

SPOTLIGHT WORD: _____

1. strategy _____

2. alertness _____

3. release _____

4. rotate _____

5. warning _____

6. foster _____

7. monotonous _____

8. courteous _____

9. generalization _____

10. manage _____

16. MELODRAMA MATRIX

Here's a two-part puzzle for word sleuths. First find each of the words defined below. As a clue, we've hidden each word in the matrix of letters you see here, in the approximate order in which they're defined. (The words may be found horizontally, vertically, or diagonally, so look hard.) As you identify each word, write it in its appropriately numbered space in the little melodrama we've written for your enjoyment—as corny a melodrama as you're likely to find, we'll warrant.

```
X X K L A X O N S I M U L T A N E O U S A
C X X U R B A N E X X V I R T U A L X X S
A X P F S P O I L S X X Q I X X M A X M S
T X H I N T E R L A N D U U X X O R F O E
A X A A X J L X T X X C I M X X R T A D S
C F L S X A U E X E H L D V U L P I N E S
L A A C G P S X G A D O A I X E H C D R E
Y R N O O E I X N A X U T R X X O U A A D
S C X X A X V K X X C T E A X X U L N T U
M I X A D V E R S A R Y C T X X S A G E R
I C X X I R G A M B I T X E X X X T O X C
C A R E E N X X A P O C A L Y P S E X O H
X L X D E P L O Y G A R G A N T U A N F I
F O R M I D A B L E X X X C O R D O N F N
P A R A D O X R A U C O U S H A W K I S H
```

31. an electrically operated noisemaker
9. stopped in early stages of its development
30. occurring at the same time
8. get totally rid of
32. a group of three people
33. determined the size of
12. extremely destructive
14. smooth mannered
16. for all practical purposes
23. not having a clear-cut organization
17. a massive organization of people, generally in rows

2. total failure
26. rewards
24. speak clearly about
10. to make less drastic
7. not part of the big city
3. hard to define precisely
1. wild dance
39. something mocking or amusing
11. something passed on from one generation to another
34. persuasive influence
38. absurd, laughable
5. desire strongly

18. tricky
37. to stimulate or prod
28. to make demands
21. enemy
20. to compete with
19. ragamuffin
36. calculated moves
15. sway from side to side
4. the end of the world

35. send into battle
25. huge
22. causing fear or awe
29. blockade
13. a puzzle that seems self-contradictory
27. harsh, noisy, disorderly
6. warlike

A Melodrama Entitled "The Dance that Wasn't, or The (1)_____ (2)_____."

Would the (3)_____ (4)_____ (5)_____ after by (6)_____ ne'er-do-wells from the (7)_____, finally (8)_____ all semblance of civilization in the school? Could it, instead, be (9)_____ or turned toward something more (10)_____ so as to leave a (11)_____ less (12)_____? That was the (13)_____ facing Super Syntax—super-hero disguised as an (14)_____ senior English teacher—as he sped out of his office to (15)_____ past a (16)_____ (17)_____ of (18)_____ (19)_____(s). He knew that he was about to (20)_____ with an (21)_____ so (22)_____, yet so (23)_____, that he could scarcely (24)_____ to his faithful friend and companion, who fell in step with Super Syntax, the (25)_____ (26)_____ the (27)_____ mob of crazed students might (28)_____ before he could effectively (29)_____ the lunch room.

(30)_____ with the sounding of the (31)_____, the dashing duo was joined by Coach, and together the (32)_____ (33)_____ what (34)_____ they could (35)_____, what (36)_____ they could use to (37)_____ the mob with.

However, as Super Syntax flung open the lunchroom door, he recalled that in reality, he'd been all along just a (38)_____ character in this (39)_____.

17. SUBSTITUTIONS #1

How quickly can you choose the best substitute for each word in italics, from the words we offer?

1. I'm not sure what effect the teacher's *admonitions* can have on the student's work.
   (a) complaints (b) corrections (c) warnings (d) grades

2. My opponent showed a *cardinal* lack of frankness.
   (a) red (b) frightening (c) deep (d) important

3. It's possible for handgun enthusiasts to *circumvent* a law.
   (a) detour around (b) trick (c) defy (d) circulate

4. The ambassador said, "We are not seeking *confrontation."*
   (a) a clash of ideas (b) a palaver (c) trouble (d) defeat

5. Her *denunciation* of her colleague almost got her fired.
   (a) accusation (b) discouragement (c) abandonment (d) delivery

6. His actions were *detrimental* to his interests.
   (a) hidden (b) harmful (c) a throwaway (d) helpful

7. The several agencies involved have *divergent* views.
   (a) troublesome (b) wishful (c) differing (d) running

8. A law has been passed *effectively* limiting the sale of cigarettes.
   (a) absolutely (b) substantially (c) necessarily (d) wishfully

9. The *stagnation* of the economy has made bankers nervous.
   (a) running away (b) inactivity (c) warring (d) warranty

10. The prospect of trouble *galvanized* the town's deputies.
    (a) frightened (b) polarized (c) incited to action (d) polished off

11. Among the union's *grievances* was the hiring of too many new personnel.
    (a) unhappinesses (b) discussions (c) causes (d) findings

12. A spirit of unity and purpose *infused* the members.
    (a) filled (b) united (c) wired (d) sundered

13. Experts blamed the war on Argentina's *intransigence.*
    (a) compliance (b) not moving (c) uncaring (d) refusal to compromise

14. The first pioneers were all rugged *individualists.*
    (a) people (b) self-reliants (c) loners (d) fighters

15. The posters reflect the *animosity* between the two groups.
    (a) resentment (b) difference (c) love (d) hole

16. They're more in the mood for *lamentation* than for celebration.
    (a) loving (b) moaning (c) speaking (d) running

17. An *entrepreneur* announced that he was bringing computers to town.
    (a) investor (b) candidate (c) executive (d) owner

18. Since he's going to have *mammoth* deficits, he's *muted* his horror at unbalanced books.
    (a) animal, forgotten (b) hidden, overlooked (c) huge, toned down (d) wasteful, dumb

19. Nine out of ten endorse *nostrums* like "more respect for authority" and "more family ties."
    (a) cure-alls (b) doubtful remedies (c) enigmas (d) parables

20. When it came to buying the cat, he became an *obstructionist*.
    (a) endorser (b) roadblock (c) troublemaker (d) candidate

18. FOCUS ON IDIOMS

An idiom is a group of words that, put together, mean something different from what they mean separately. Among the words in the left-hand column are ten idioms. Circle the two words that *aren't* idioms, and then match them all with their closest synonyms in the right-hand column.

1. ex cathedra	a. form a restrictive line
2. shore up	b. instead of
3. trumped up	c. rumored in many places
4. quantum leap	d. bring to light
5. in lieu of	e. support
6. bruited about	f. abrupt change
7. crocodile tears	g. with authority
8. cordon off	h. take over
9. ad lib	i. perform without preparation
10. seriocomic	j. a show of false sorrow
11. co-opt	k. combining serious and comic elements
12. fob off	l. untruthfully put together
13. ferret out	m. support
14. buoy up	n. pass off as genuine

19. STRONG ROOTS

Many English words are rooted in Latin. If you understand the meaning of the Latin root, you can often figure out the meaning of the word. But can you figure out the word from its meaning? (To help, we list all the words at the end.)

Root	Meaning	English word's meaning	Word?
vocare	to call	(1) calling forth anger	_____
		(2) a call for help	_____
fundus	bottom	(3) to sink to the bottom	_____
		(4) almost bottomless	_____
litigium	dispute	(5) prone to dispute	_____
		(6) a legal dispute	_____
haerere	to stick	(7) holding together logically	_____
		(8) lacking consistency	_____
ped	foot	(9) ambling unimaginatively	_____
		(10) a charge of walkers	_____
malus	bad	(11) hatred, bad feeling	_____
		(12) to speak evil of	_____
praeceps	headlong	(13) rushing headlong	_____
		(14) very edge	_____
acer	sharp	(15) sharply bitter	_____
		(16) bitter anger	_____
vertere	to turn	(17) one turned against you	_____
		(18) a bad turn of fortune	_____
circulus	circle	(19) to walk around; avoid	_____
		(20) careful to look around	_____

Words to choose from: acrid, acrimony, adversary, adversity, circumspect, circumvent, cohesive, founder, incoherent, invocation, litigation, litigious, malice, malign, pedestrian, precipice, precipitate, profound, provocative, stampede.

20. PROS AND CONS

All the words referred to in these clues contain either *pro* or *con*. Can you figure them out? (Be careful. A few hide their pros and cons in the middle.) For a real challenge, don't peek at the *Words to choose from*.

1. This con adjective likes argument
2. This con noun fits into its surroundings
3. This pro noun has a protector
4. This pro adjective is very deep
5. This con adjective is very sorry
6. This pro adjective is widely known
7. This con noun takes a face-to-face stand
8. This con adjective is concise
9. This pro adjective is open to question
10. This con noun happens at an embarrassing time
11. This pro verb takes someone's property
12. This con noun is pure guesswork
13. This con adjective is that way from birth
14. This pro verb breeds freely
15. This pro adjective shows an inclination, a proclivity
16. This pro noun is full of approval
17. This con adjective tries to appease everyone
18. This con noun is a chance event
19. This pro noun is a sphere of activity
20. This con adjective is unscrupulous
21. This pro verb proposes ideas
22. This con verb confuses and embarrasses
23. This pro adjective is too expensive
24. This pro noun brings a reconciliation
25. This con verb makes things blessed
26. This con verb stoops and patronizes
27. This con adjective winds and twists
28. This pro noun investigates

29. This con verb remakes things
30. This pro adjective is very suggestive

Words to choose from: approbation, expropriate, probe, problematic, profound, proliferate, prohibitive, prominent, propensity, propound, protégé, province, provocative, rapprochement, conciliatory, condescend, confrontation, congenital, conjecture, consecrate, contentious, context, contingency, contretemps, contrite, convoluted, disconcert, laconic, reconstitute, unconscionable.

21. MEET THE PRESS #2

All these sentences come straight from one news article in the popular press. Would you understand it all?

1. Amid the forests of the Florida Everglades, Cuban exiles once plotted to *oust* Fidel Castro.
   (a) kill (b) rout (c) overthrow (d) rob

2. This time the rebels were Nicaraguan *expatriates*.
   (a) envoys (b) patriots (c) sympathizers (d) exiles

3. Newsmen saw *simulated* assaults through mud and underbrush.
   (a) planned (b) simple (c) imitation (d) copies

4. Gonzalez climbed atop a wooden *podium* and explained what these maneuvers *portended* for the hated governments.
   (a) pedestal, aimed (b) platform, signified
   (c) footstool, pretended (d) truck, carried

5. When it comes to pointed questions, he's *evasive*.
   (a) outspoken (b) avoiding direct answers (c) tricky (d) moody

6. Will he disclose the location of two training camps that he *purportedly* runs in Florida?
   (a) supposedly (b) single-handedly (c) purposefully
   (d) preparedly

7. How about a visit to his *putative* paratrooper school?
   (a) assumed to exist (b) punishing (c) golf course
   (d) nonexistent

8. The reporter left, and life returned to its normal *languor*.
   (a) weakness (b) long days (c) listlessness (d) meaning

9. The reporter brought home Gonzalez's *plethora* of incredible claims.
   (a) sackful (b) excess (c) level (d) manual

10. In San Salvador, the late afternoon heat was *sweltering*.
    (a) heat-prostrating (b) suffocating (c) well-to-do
    (d) making welts

11. The shots were *inevitable* reminders of the *strife* that rages through the tiny country.
    (a) unlikely, rain (b) unwelcome, tyranny (c) avoidable, battle
    (d) unavoidable, struggle

12. Threats of death *vied* with leaflets and posters as tools of political persuasion.
    (a) competed (b) lied (c) tied (c) lived

13. The assembly is to frame a new constitution and name an *interim* president.
    (a) interested (b) temporary (c) lifetime (d) fair

14. Leftist groups are *boycotting* the election.
    (a) sending boys (b) sending cots (c) sending voters
    (d) refusing to send voters

15. The guerrilla *insurgency* has *escalated* in the past year.
    (a) instigation, climbed (b) rush, decreased
    (c) mini-revolution, intensified (d) instance, scabbed

16. Will enough voters turn out to give the results any real *legitimacy*?
    (a) legality (b) weight (c) difference (d) notice

17. There is considerable public skepticism in this country where elections have been *manipulated* since 1931.
    (a) handled (b) controlled unfairly (c) managed (d) going on

18. Bombs and guns *intimidate* the people so they do not go out and vote.
    (a) threaten (b) pen in (c) frustrate (d) warn

19. Top officials expected a major rebel *offensive*, but guerrillas launched only a handful of *probes*.
    (a) blaspheme, rods (b) march, warnings
    (c) attack, investigative efforts (d) faux pas, robberies

20. Then a group of *insurgents* opened fire on a funeral.
    (a) uprisings (b) revolutionaries (c) scoundrels (d) dogs

21. The war is being financed by *expatriate oligarchs.*
(a) *overseas businessmen (b) exiled supporters of the small group in power (c) small outlaw groups*
(d) *patriotic enemies of the throne*

22. He has been accused of plotting to overthrow the *junta.*
(a) *government (b) rebels (c) ruling committee (d) jute growers*

23. The junta's leader went on the *hustings* with his message.
(a) *radio (b) television (c) campaign circuit (d) hinterlands*

24. He's making efforts to *moderate* his image.
(a) *tone down (b) belie (c) mediate (d) outdistance*

25. Meanwhile, Washington was seeking to *shore up* the beleaguered forces of moderation, and to answer all charges with a *perfunctory* "no comment."
(a) *wash ashore, quick (b) tie up, perfect (c) light up, dull*
(d) *bolster, mechanical*

22. IN A WORD

Some English words have been derived by putting two good words together. Others only look like that's the way they evolved. Were all the following words in the left-hand column originally two words? For each word, circle Y for yes and N for no. Then match each word with its meaning.

	Originally 2 words?		
1. aftermath	Y N	a.	from outside the earth
2. backlash	Y N	b.	most basic element
3. chestnut	Y N	c.	result
4. logjam	Y N	d.	mix of serious and funny
5. overarching	Y N	e.	strong negative reaction
6. belie	Y N	f.	all-embracing
7. cornerstone	Y N	g.	stale story
8. beset	Y N	h.	impasse
9. seriocomic	Y N	i.	trouble or set upon
10. extraterrestrial	Y N	j.	contradict

23. MAKE-A-WORD #1

The letters of the highlighted word appear, in order, represented by an *x* in each of the words defined below. With the definitions and number of letters in each blank given as clues, how fast can you fill in the highlighted word—and use it to find the rest of the defined words?

_____ *(a word meaning the limits within which one's authority may be exercised)*

1. deadlock or impasse
   ____ __ __
   (3) x (2)

2. full of joy
   __ __ ____
   (1) x (6)

3. secret dialect
   __ __ ___
   (1) x (3)

4. gift recipient
   ____ __ ____
   (4) x (5)

5. tilted to one side
   __ ____
   x (5)

6. false appearance
   ____ __ __
   (4) x (1)

7. total failure
   __ __ ___
   (1) x (4)

8. done through habit
   __ ____
   x (6)

9. stop early on
   ____ __
   (4) x

10. debt settlement
    _____ __ __
    (8)   x (2)

11. heat up for growth
    __ __ ___
    (1) x (4)

12. shard
    _____ __ __
    (6)   x (1)

24. ONION CROSSWORD

We call this crossword puzzle *Onion* because it uses only *an, en, in, on,* and *un* words from the vocabulary list.

Across

1. intensely disliked
5. mischievous youngster
7. no clear attitude: _____ committal
8. using so few words as to seem rude
9. to destroy
11. someone cursed
13. a group within a larger group
16. having little chance of getting relief
19. having no name
21. a representative from one country to another
25. official papers that support a claim
28. invisible now, but able to be made visible
29. extremely idealistic

Down

1. expression that shows similarities between things
2. same as 8 across
3. attaching one thing onto another
4. someone who is intensely disliked
6. an introductory action
10. flowing in
12. something that soothes
14. break into parts
15. showing very warm feelings
17. very, very poor
18. completely filled with or affected by something
20. words around a passage that affect its overall meaning
22. something very difficult to explain
23. to cut away unwanted parts
24. to baffle
26. full of joy: jubi————
27. not looking healthy

25. HORS D'OEUVRES

Hors d'oeuvres are little snacks served before the meal. Since the verbs in the left-hand column all end in *ate*, we're serving them up as hors d'oeuvres. See if you can match them with their synonyms in the right-hand column before the dinner bell rings.

1. alleviate	a. accomplish
2. incinerate	b. erase
3. differentiate	c. repeat
4. negotiate	d. penetrate
5. extrapolate	e. discriminate
6. obliterate	f. project
7. postulate	g. branch
8. fluctuate	h. propose
9. formulate	i. deviate
10. reiterate	j. guess
11. pullulate	k. hasten
12. permeate	l. waver
13. simulate	m. relieve
14. bifurcate	n. swarm
15. manipulate	o. compose
16. speculate	p. feign
17. aberrate	q. burn
18. articulate	r. fasten
19. precipitate	s. use

26. DOUBLE THREAT

The words defined below make a word chain in which the last two letters of each word are also the first two letters of the word that follows. How quickly can you complete the chain? To start you off, we provide the first and last two letters in the chain.

1. to be in the same place at the same time   co_____
2. gets worse or goes wrong   _____
3. heightens in amount or intensity   _____
4. preferring to forget reality or routine   _____
5. headlong rush of people or animals   _____
6. expressing scorn   _____
7. having the qualities of spring   _____
8. one who is unselfishly devoted to others   _____
9. to brand, especially as shameful   _____
10. one who is fanatically devoted to a cause   _____ ot

27. THEATER TALK

Let's try a little talk about the theater.

1. The play is a musical about a hero who tries several *ploys* to win the hand of a woman named Yum Yum.
   (a) arguments (b) attempts (c) tricks (d) Hawaiian foods

2. The Lord High Executioner's speeches are filled with *rhetoric*.
   (a) conviction (b) fancy words (c) knowledge (d) enthusiasm

3. The backdrop consists of artists' *renderings* of Japan.
   (a) oils (b) representations (c) tear-outs (d) give-aways

4. Koko *proscribes* several modern villains in his song "I've Got a Little List."
   (a) sentences to death (b) advises (c) lists (d) suggests

5. Gilbert and Sullivan's plays always include at least one *garrulous* character.
   (a) strangled (b) poor (c) gaudy (d) big-mouthed

6. There are only two *gaffes* in the entire production.
   (a) stagehands (b) blunders (c) rude remarks (d) miscues

7. There is a song about the *calamitous* adventure of a bird who sings tit-willow.
   (a) sorrowful (b) turbulent (c) calming (d) disastrous

8. The musical contains several *farcical* episodes.
   (a) absurd (b) idiotic (c) fanciful (d) farfetched

9. The performers always insert several *ad libs.*
   (a) jokes (b) censored remarks (c) improvements
   (d) improvisations

10. The program for the performance will be kept among our *memorabilia.*
    (a) memories (b) mementos (c) memoirs (d) memos

28. SUBSTITUTIONS #2

Test your understanding of these sentences that appeared in a newsmagazine.

1. Some 96 million Americans fuss, cuss, and struggle with *sheaves* of tax forms.
   (a) bundles (b) lists (c) piles (d) wrappers

2. This typographic tangle has *proliferated* since the 16th Amendment.
   (a) perforated (b) been preserved (c) multiplied (d) gone on

3. There are *myriad* laws, rules, and regulations to observe.
   (a) murky (b) many (c) mighty (d) mixed-up

4. The tax form covers every *eventuality* from property losses to lottery prizes.
   (a) difficulty (b) event (c) deduction (d) possibility

5. Press coverage has improved with the *influx* of old pros such as Peter Arnett.
   (a) inflow (b) introduction (c) changing around (d) talent

6. *The New York Times* characterized the *factions* in succinct articles.
   (a) subgroups (b) factories (c) factors (d) actions

7. The paper's editor *instituted* a cleaner, livelier layout.
   (a) taught (b) established (c) housed (d) offered

8. His insistence on rapid change *nettled* some staff veterans.
   (a) comforted (b) punctured (c) caught (d) annoyed

9. Murdock cannot *sack* the editor without approval of the directors.
   (a) bag (b) fire (c) hire (d) heave

10. He's said to be bound to silence by his *severance* agreement.
    (a) cutting (b) missing (c) separating (d) harsh

11. The *mercurial* Evans is a product of the working class.
    (a) changeable (b) touchy (c) quick-witted (d) brilliant

12. In a speech, he *lauded* Evans' contribution.
    (a) applauded (b) legitimized (c) seconded (d) spoke of

13. The *bifurcated* outcome, containing bad news for both sides, was probably the result of a compromise by the jury.
    (a) halfhearted (b) double-edged (c) two-sectioned (d) awful

14. James Earl Jones, the *magnific* actor now playing Othello, was married at age 51.
    (a) well-built (b) very tall (c) magical (d) magnificent

15. There are *scatological* scenes that Richard Pryor might envy, but too often the shocks and surprises are *gratuitous*.
    (a) obscene, uncalled-for (b) shocking, ungracious
    (c) comedy, to pay a debt (d) runaway, too much

16. No detail is too *gross* to be recorded.
    (a) heavy (b) vulgar (c) untimely (d) picky

17. His *residual* pride prevents him from putting *euphemisms* between himself and his experience.
    (a) left-handed, words (b) sticky, kind words
    (c) remaining, pretty words (d) dry, pleasure

18. The book is filled with *mordant* memories.
    (a) sharp (b) dying (c) unhappy (d) plentiful

19. The Germans saw in Hitler the *apotheosis* of their history.
    (a) most sacred instance (b) most perfect example
    (c) central figure (d) apathy

20. The author is a connoisseur of the *raffish*, the *macabre* and the *sleazy*.
    (a) floating, strange, poorly made (b) doggerel, dance, ugly
    (c) rakish, bony, slippery (d) unconventional, weird, shoddy

29. BATTLE PLAN

Match these words of war with their synonyms.

1. strife	a. peace
2. boycott	b. hatred
3. contention	c. uprising
4. unilateral	d. battle
5. vendetta	e. civvies
6. cataclysm	f. catastrophe
7. blitzkrieg	g. raid
8. spoils	h. stronghold
9. detente	i. warlike
10. bastion	j. one-sided
11. malice	k. war
12. kamikaze	l. encounter
13. insurgence	m. feud
14. bellicose	n. self-destructive
15. internecine	o. placement
16. mufti	p. blacklist
17. deployment	q. bombardment
18. hawk	r. warmonger
19. confrontation	s. booty
20. foray	t. fratricidal

30. LOADED LANGUAGE

You can put a great deal of meaning into one word—if you know the word. Can you find the missing word in each sentence?

1. That's a _____ car. *(of lasting value)*
2. The play was a poor _____ for her talents. *(means of display)*

3. Two things were happening _____. *(at one and the same time)*

4. The two parties have to _____ the agreement. *(formally approve)*

5. If you water that plant, it may be _____. *(brought back to life)*

6. The art exhibit was a Chagall _____. *(all his past work)*

7. Sparrows are _____ in England. *(everywhere at once)*

8. The thieves figured out a _____ for the robbery. *(plan for what was to happen)*

9. Her ideas ran the _____ from silly to brilliant. *(continuous range)*

10. _____, he left the door open. *(through accidental oversight)*

11. Those words _____ the conservative way of thinking. *(are a typical example of)*

12. Our meeting was a _____ that we both wanted to forget. *(embarrassing occurrence)*

13. _____ speaking, the Mississippi is a river of gold. *(substituting a word to show a second idea)*

14. They declared a _____ on arms shipment. *(a temporary suspension of activity)*

15. That thesis is just _____ acceptable. *(near the lower limits)*

16. The policy has a _____ that makes us responsible for accidents in the street. *(denial of legal responsibility)*

17. You've shown an _____ lack of respect. *(never having happened before)*

18. The paint job was purely _____. *(correcting just surface defects)*

19. The _____ for Scantily Clad Attendants is SCAT. *(word made of the first letters of several words)*

20. Before we moved, we _____ all our property. *(turned into cash)*

Words to choose from: metaphorically, scenario, inadvertently, retrospective, cosmetic, simultaneously, resuscitated, marginally, unprecedented, acronym, ubiquitous, spectrum, vintage, vehicle, moratorium, liquidated, exemplify, disclaimer, contretemps, ratify.

31. THE ANIMAL KINGDOM

1. What word describes both a daytime bird of prey and a warmonger?

2. What word describes an insect pest and, when you add a *b,* means to suggest a topic?

3. What word is a male deer and, when an entire country is added, means inaction?

4. What large lizard, when it's crying, means feigned emotion?

5. Add *imilate* to a donkey for a word meaning absorb.

6. Add *ble* to a young pigeon to get a noisy argument.

7. This word is both a pheasant-like game bird and a complaint.

8. Add *irant* to the snake that bit Cleopatra for a word meaning a political candidate.

9. This red bird is also indispensable.

10. To a male sheep, add *ification* to get a consequence.

11. This word describes both a young bird and an inexperienced person.

12. Add *in* to a mongrel dog to lay oneself open to trouble.

13. This extinct elephant also means huge.

14. Add *gr* to that Egyptian snake to achieve understanding.

15. This polecat also means to search out.

16. Add *ess* to the donkey to evaluate it.

17. One of the lobes on a whale's tail is also a stroke of luck.

18. Add *aste* to a baby sheep to punish verbally.

19. Add *s* and *ding* to what a cow chews to describe things blown by the wind.

20. Put together a mongrel dog and its tail to cut this game short.

32. HOW VERBAL ARE YOU #2

Can you choose just the right verb to express what you mean? Try your hand at finding the verbs defined below—without peeking at the *Words to choose from.*

1. to give a false impression *(5 letters beginning with f)*

2. to report a rumor in several places *(10 letters beginning with b)*

3. to lessen someone's pain or bad feeling *(7 letters beginning with a)*

4. to take up and support a cause *(7 letters beginning with e)*

5. to forfeit a contest through failure to perform *(7 letters beginning with d)*

6. to conclude on the basis of guesswork *(10 letters beginning with c)*

7. to turn to one's own economic advantage *(7 letters beginning with e)*

8. to bring to light by searching *(9 letters beginning with f)*

9. to bring out a response *(6 letters beginning with e)*

10. to form a restrictive line around something *(9 letters beginning with c)*

11. to cut short *(7 letters beginning with c)*

12. to add to what's already there *(7 letters beginning with a)*

13. to provoke hostility *(10 letters beginning with a)*

14. to demand as being needed and wanted *(5 letters beginning with e)*

15. to clear from blame *(9 letters beginning with e)*

16. to persuade against an action *(8 letters beginning with d)*

17. to polish until it shines *(7 letters beginning with b)*

18. to mix together different elements *(10 letters beginning with a)*

19. to get along *(4 letters beginning with f)*

20. to perform without preparation *(5 letters beginning with a)*

Words to choose from: ad lib, amalgamate, antagonize, assuage, augment, bruit about, burnish, conjecture, cordon off, curtail, default, dissuade, elicit, espouse, exact, exonerate, exploit, fare, feign, ferret out.

33. THIRD SPOTLIGHT

Once again we'll spotlight a word with an interesting past. This one goes back to Greek mythology and describes the messenger of the gods, who was also the god of commerce, eloquence, science, and thievery. As you can imagine, he was a god of many constantly changing moods. We use his name today as an adjective to describe an inconstant or changeable person, a person born under his sign, or a person who shows his eloquence, ingenuity, or thievishness. Fill in the adjective; its letters are, in order, the first letter of every word defined below.

1. early _____
2. eccentric _____
3. dissonant _____
4. take over _____
5. unsoftened _____
6. list _____
7. unweighable _____
8. receiver _____
9. penalization _____

34. IN-TELLIGENCE TEST

Each word defined below begins with the letters *in*. How many can you get right without peeking at the *Words to choose from*?

1. relating to torched property; tending to inflame
2. made legally ineligible; disabled
3. the very embodiment of a particular quality
4. severe poverty
5. to burn to cinders
6. unable to be broken apart
7. accidental
8. poor judgment in how one acts or speaks
9. to bring on oneself
10. cleverness in designing
11. inrush
12. lack of competence
13. independent thinker
14. to prod forward
15. completely filled
16. motivated to act
17. not satisfiable
18. nonchalant

19. unavoidable

20. attempting to win favor

21. unfairness

22. talent for taking action

23. well-deserved bad reputation

24. seemingly forever

25. interfere in another country's affairs

26. forming a basic part

27. accustomed to the undesirable

28. mutually destructive

29. going where one isn't wanted

30. insinuation of bad reputation

Words to choose from: inadvertent, incapacitated, incarnation, incendiary, incinerate, incur, indigence, indiscretion, indissoluble, individualist, ineptitude, inequity, inevitable, infamy, influx, infused, ingenuity, ingratiating, initiative, innuendo, insatiable, insouciant, inspired, instigate, integral, interminably, internecine, intervene, intrusive, inured.

35. SCRAMBLED MAXIMS #2

Fill in the correct word for each definition and the first letters, read in sequence, will make up the first and last halves of two *maxims,* or wise sayings. Elsewhere among our *Scrambled Maxims* you'll find the missing halves of both maxims. To start you off, we've filled in a definition. But try not to peek at *Words to choose from* until you must.

1. a small tax _____

2. an election platform _____

3. opening a new era _____

4. relating to war _____

5. urgent need _____

6. key element _____

7. manifestation _____

8. dispense with _____

9. state of being an essential component   _____

10. permissive   _____

11. to become fixed in a place   _____

12. overabundance   _____

13. luminous   _____

14. shocking   _____

15. 52 weeks   <u>year</u>_____

16. to practice or engage in   _____

17. yearning   _____

18. encourage   _____

19. foolish   _____

20. arm of the sea   _____

21. amusement   _____

22. bunkum   _____

23. stability   _____

24. plot outline   _____

25. unqualified   _____

26. provoked   _____

27. rough fragment   _____

28. theoretical   _____

29. self-contradictory   _____

30. offering no indication of attitude   _____

31. to impose or extort   _____

32. loud spilling and hitting sound   _____

Words to choose from: epochal, cornerstone, lax, appalling, inspire, equilibrium, nettled, ironic, hustings, immediacy, integral, lustrous, hankering, hokum, unmitigated, hypothetical, exact, noncommittal, ludicrous, lodge, epiphany, estuary, splat, shard, scenario, titillation, wage, plethora, waive, martial, tithe.

36. AFTER-DINNER TALK

Here's a game to play after dinner, since all the verbs in the left-hand column end in the letters *ate*. Can you match them correctly with their *antonyms* (meaning *opposites*) in the right-hand column?

1. abate		a.	rebuke
2. annihilate		b.	purify
3. consecrate		c.	intensify
4. incapacitate		d.	activate
5. terminate		e.	refresh
6. permeate		f.	divide
7. reinstate		g.	profane
8. instigate		h.	establish
9. interrogate		i.	dissuade
10. repudiate		j.	expel
11. adulterate		k.	diminish
12. escalate		l.	incriminate
13. adulate		m.	enable
14. proliferate		n.	answer
15. assimilate		o.	remove
16. exonerate		p.	begin
17. stagnate		q.	emanate
18. intimidate		r.	protect
19. degenerate		s.	adopt
20. dessicate		t.	improve

37. AD STUMPER

Most ads are written so that a 6-year-old can read them. But every once in a while we come across one that challenges our intelligence. These sentences come straight from a Mobil Oil Company ad. Choose the best synonym for each italicized word.

1. In the minds of some *pseudo* astronomers, this rare configuration of planets *augured* that celestial forces would propel us all into the blackness of outer space.
   (a) silly, warned (b) unnamed, meant (c) phony, predicted
   (d) foot-dragging, wagered

2. For millions around the globe, life is a heart-rending journey toward an elusive *apocalypse* which refuses to arrive in time to end their suffering.
   (a) trip to heaven (b) epoch (c) millennium (d) euphoria

3. Medical researchers cling to threads of clinical evidence with only a *miniscule* chance that they will save a life years hence.
   (a) minister's (b) half-way (c) tiny (d) happy

4. Some of life's ingredients are quite *pedestrian*.
   (a) ordinary (b) slow (c) walking (d) dull

5. Chemicals that provide creature comforts are within the grasp of human *ingenuity*.
   (a) genius (b) inventiveness (c) use (d) engines

6. When products become scarce—*by dint of* nature's whims— their shortage reflects itself in economic suffering, sometimes of *cataclysmic* proportions.
   (a) besides, overwhelming (b) bent by, uneven
   (c) due to, overwhelming (d) because of, unfortunate

7. Political *squabbling* interferes with the delivery of life's *prerequisites*.
   (a) dealing, results (b) quarreling, requirements
   (c) infighting, needs (d) dining, perks

8. We're fearful that the *millennium* would spell the end of human challenge.
   (a) world's end (b) 21st century (c) year of peace
   (d) time in paradise

9. Serious scientists *postulate* that the solar system may disintegrate in a few billion years.
   (a) post notice (b) possess (c) claim (d) wish

10. It gives us time to think *coherently* about the *efficacy* of war as a way of settling things.
    (a) truthfully, efficiency (b) carefully, effort
    (c) strongly, silliness (d) logically, effectiveness

38. LOOK-ALIKES

Some words look just enough alike that, if we read quickly or listen inattentively, they can be confused. See if you know which means which.

1. (a) profound, (b) propound   (1) deep-felt, (2) propose
2. (a) flounder, (b) founder   (1) to sink, (2) a fish
3. (a) diverge, (b) divert   (1) differ, (2) distract
4. (a) punitive, (b) putative   (1) supposed, (2) retaliatory
5. (a) demean, (b) demeanor   (1) disgrace, (2) behavior
6. (a) oblige, (b) oblique   (1) obligate, (2) devious
7. (a) paradigm, (b) paradox   (1) dilemma, (2) model
8. (a) renounce, (b) renown   (1) eminence, (2) relinquish
9. (a) specter, (b) spectrum   (1) range, (2) spirit
10. (a) instigate, (b) institute   (1) incite, (2) begin
11. (a) irreverent, (b) irrelevant   (1) unrelated, (2) disrespectful
12. (a) parity, (b) parody   (1) imitation, (2) equality
13. (a) implacable, (b) impeccable   (1) perfect, (2) unyielding
14. (a) abate, (b) abort   (1) lessen, (2) stop
15. (a) transient, (b) transcendent   (1) fleeting, (2) surpassing
16. (a) entity, (b) entitlement   (1) thing, (2) claims support
17. (a) malice, (b) malign   (1) hatred, (2) harmful
18. (a) ramification, (b) ratification   (1) approval, (2) outgrowth
19. (a) shrewd, (b) skewed   (1) tricky, (2) slanted
20. (a) straggle, (b) strangle   (1) choke, (2) stray

39. ANTY MATTER

All the words described in the following sentences contain *ant*. Do you know the words?

1. The woman jumped for joy. She was j_____ant.
2. The ape is huge. He is g_____ant_____.
3. The statement is very much to the point. It is r_____ant.

4. You must take back your words. R_____ant!

5. Computer science has progressed greatly. It was a q_____ant_____ leap.

6. His behavior is abnormal. It's a_____ant.

7. That's too high a price. It's e_____ant.

8. I've got a great liking for good music. It's a strong p_____ant.

9. She was one of the hopefuls in the Miss America contest. She was an a_____ant.

10. Look at his bright red hat. It certainly is f_____ant.

11. That has nothing to do with the matter. It's i_____ant.

12. The contest sponsor raised the amount of the prize. He upped the ant_____.

13. The play affected me deeply. It was p_____ant.

14. Don't oppose him. He doesn't like to be ant_____.

15. I couldn't change the child's mind. He remained a_____ant.

16. That was an impudent remark. It was i_____ant.

17. He spoke offensively loud. It was a b_____ant attempt for the limelight.

18. The coat was just soiled. It suffered no s_____ant_____ damage.

19. The speaker used a lot of sarcasm. He displayed a m_____ant wit.

20. The leaders were triumphant, and their followers were e_____ant.

40. A FAMILY RESEMBLANCE

In each series, all but one of the words belong in the same family. Circle the word that's an outsider, and tell what the others have in common.

1. cordon off, curb, curtail, foster, prune

2. acrid, animosity, anodyne, scathing

3. bogus, spurious, duplicitous, utopian, pseudo

4. legitimate, spurious, substantive, tangible, veritable

5. enterprise, impotence, initiative, spunk
6. bastion, estuary, precipice, rendezvous, ubiquitous
7. polymath, primer, pseudonym, vehicle
8. banal, bumbling, mediocre, pedestrian, trite
9. cardinal, centenary, fiscal, troika, triumvirate, unilateral
10. hodgepodge, logjam, detritus, shard, sheaf
11. ante, collateral, legacy, levy, tithe
12. dubious, interrogate, inured, trepidation
13. formulation, methodology, miscalculation, postulate
14. ecological, heartland, hinterland, hustings, municipality
15. deftly, ineffectual, ineptitude, mediocre
16. exonerate, expropriate, pilfer, proscribe
17. blitzkrieg, incendiary, incinerate, mortification
18. jurisdiction, laud, legacy, legitimacy, litigation
19. cosmetic, facade, panacea, puffery
20. arcane, argot, latent, overt

41. MEET THE PRESS #3

All these sentences are straight out of the popular press. If you met their authors at a party, would you know what they were talking about?

1. They've found such historical *detritus* as FDR's lap robe, Nazi pilots' socks, and a banner from a John L. Sullivan fight.
   (a) memorabilia (b) ruins (c) mixture (d) additions
2. Vince *meandered* through the large, dusty room, past lost cultures and found treasures.
   (a) wandered casually (b) ran quickly (c) made his way
   (d) got lost
3. Which powers are the proper *province* of the national government and which are reserved to the states?
   (a) location (b) decision (c) function (d) persuasion
4. The President's televised performance was *vintage* Reagan, flawlessly paced and forcefully persuasive.
   (a) fine quality (b) outdated (c) obsolete (d) new style

47

5. He has long been *nurturing* the seeds of federalism.
   (a) hiding (b) harvesting (c) blowing (d) developing

6. The advisor has been searching for a *vehicle* to regain domina
   tion of the political debate.
   (a) device (b) automobile (c) trick (d) courier

7. The Senator was unlikely to be *diverted* by the committee's
   grandiose plan.
   (a) thrilled, huge (b) turned aside, wishful
   (c) cajoled, wishy-washy (d) distracted, pompous

8. There are too many *imponderables* for anyone to predict *deficits* or surpluses with any degree of accuracy.
   (a) unthinkable thoughts, disadvantages
   (b) heavy items, minuses (c) unweighable things, shortages
   (d) airy ideas, losses

9. One of their *implicit* goals is to *cap* or reduce social spending.
   (a) thoughtful, top (b) unhesitating, keep from rising
   (c) unquestioned, cork up (d) suggested, stop

10. The plan *foundered* on the rocks of the committee system.
    (a) fished (b) sank (c) washed up (d) floated

11. The fathers of these social programs will not be at all eager to
    see them *terminated.*
    (a) ended (b) bridged (c) locked up (d) dead

12. The Democrats are expected to make political capital of the
    perceived unfairness of his progams for the poor.
    (a) obvious (b) suspected (c) noticed (d) subjective

13. Nobody quarreled with his *professed* goals.
    (a) stated (b) lying (c) desirable (d) candid

14. His real motives were not as *altruistic* as those he set forth.
    (a) true (b) all-encompassing (c) devoted (d) unselfish

15. She *fobbed it off* on the states, expecting it would die there.
    (a) wished it (b) passed it off (c) inflicted it (d) watched it go

16. Cities are pitted against state capitals as all *jockey* to protect
    their own economic interests.
    (a) fight (b) race (c) maneuver (d) work

17. Only a federal presence can hold down the *inequities* stemming
    from unwillingness to deal fairly with the problem.
    (a) troubles (b) tenacity (c) unfair results (d) uncaring results

18. The primary *rationale* seems to be convenience.
    (a) result (b) explanation (c) difficulty (d) trick

19. They scurried off to their computers to determine just how they would *fare* in dollars.
    (a) get along (b) eat (c) pay off (d) get paid
20. If the swap is approved, the estimated *disparities* will be large.
    (a) disrepair (b) despair (c) differences (d) losses

42. SCRAMBLED MAXIMS #3

The first letters of each defined word, read from top to bottom, make up the first and last halves of two maxims. Elsewhere among our *Scrambled Maxims* are the missing halves of both maxims. To start you off, we've filled in a definition. Try not to peek at *Words to choose from*.

1. to nourish   _____
2. red-yellow color   _____
3. hesitant, irresolute   _____
4. apparent   _____
5. indirectly   _____
6. place or stead   _____
7. dying   _____
8. one of a ruling group   _____
9. patent medicine   _____
10. suicidal   _____
11. to take advantage of   _____
12. quick hard pull   <u>yank</u>_____
13. obviously harmful   _____
14. out in the open   _____

Words to choose from: detrimental, exploit, faltering, lieu, kamikaze, moribund, nostrum, nurture, obliquely, ocher, oligarch, overt, ostensibly.

43. DESULTORY CROSSWORD

We call this a desultory crossword puzzle as a warning not to look for any well-defined plan as to whether a set of letters forms a word or not. All you can go by are the numbers and the definitions below.

Across

1. spread gossip *(2 words)*
5. said of overused expressions
8. lacking firmness
10. word introducing hypothetical statement
11. when two ideas agree they ____cide
12. to fight for superiority
15. by vested authority *(2 words):* _____ ____edra
16. loud or very conspicuous
17. was typical of: exemplif____
18. because of *(3 words):* by _____ of
20. what one does at a food orgy
22. prefix meaning not
23. holding together well
27. wander en route
29. hinterland building
30. clothing
33. suspended judgment
34. float
37. edge of a precipice
39. to chair: moder____

40. hardened into acceptance
41. central region
43. turn and turn and turn
46. no anathema for skiers
47. silly, childish

Down

1. stumbling or stuttering
2. unchangeably
3. two-sided
4. attack: _____fensive
5. poison-infected
6. staple of indigent people
7. accidental oversight
9. divine human
11. act of firing: severan_____
13. flamboyant skin mark
14. violent conflict
16. verb infinitive describing an entity
19. deadlock in negotiations
21. to control, often with trickery
24. salesman's nonsense
25. 21-gun salute
26. device for displaying one's talents
27. overly sentimental
28. shortfall or loss
31. keen sight
32. lodgers
34. to practice self-puffery
35. to check
36. ocher is a mixture of yellow and _____
38. warring part of a group: facti_____
42. explanation: ration_____
44. something to soothe: _____odyne
45. spoken communication: rhe_____ric

44. FOUR-LETTER WORDS

Even 4-letter words sometimes give us trouble—though they often slip by so quickly, we overlook the fact that the meaning isn't clear. Test how well you know the 4-letter words on the left by matching them with their synonyms from the list on the right.

1. curb	a.	praise
2. drab	b.	self-satisfied
3. foil	c.	wild party
4. fare	d.	rest
5. coup	e.	force
6. wage	f.	thwart
7. goad	g.	slime
8. garb	h.	master stroke
9. fete	i.	rob
10. gibe	j.	direction
11. tack	k.	unchanging
12. rift	l.	engage in
13. lieu	m.	cheer
14. oust	n.	prod
15. levy	o.	elegant
16. laud	p.	restrain
17. posh	q.	party
18. jape	r.	taunt
19. smug	s.	manage
20. sway	t.	choose
21. muck	u.	dress
22. orgy	v.	tax
23. laze	w.	power
24. cull	x.	leak
25. dint	y.	break
26. buoy	z.	tactic
27. ante	aa.	place
28. seep	bb.	mock
29. ploy	cc.	expel
30. sack	dd.	payoff

45. MAKE-A-WORD #2

The letters of the highlighted word appear, in order, where we've marked an *x* in each word below. Using the definitions and numbers of letters we've given as clues, how fast can you fill in the highlighted word—and use it to find the rest of the defined words?

_____ *(a word meaning something that proves the truth or genuineness of something else)*

1. coming from a cause

$\overline{\quad}$ *x* $\overline{\qquad\qquad}$
(1)   (4)

2. popularity

$\overline{\qquad}$ *x* $\overline{\quad}$
(3)   (1)

3. not vague

$\overline{\qquad\qquad}$ *x*
(7)

4. to sell hard and deceitfully

$\overline{\quad}$ *x* $\overline{\qquad\qquad}$
(5)

5. land just above an earthquake

$\overline{\qquad\qquad}$ *x* $\overline{\quad}$
(7)   (1)

6. to bring on oneself

$\overline{\quad}$ *x* $\overline{\qquad}$
(1)   (3)

7. explanation for what happened

$\overline{\quad}$ *x* $\overline{\qquad\qquad}$
(2)   (6)

8. emotional balance

$\overline{\qquad}$ *x* $\overline{\qquad}$
(5)   (5)

9. sympathetic involvement in another's experience

$\overline{\quad}$ *x* $\overline{\qquad\qquad}$
(2)   (6)

10. uniquely significant

$\overline{\qquad}$ *x* $\overline{\quad}$
(5)   (1)

11. to limit in fluctuation

$\overline{\quad}$ *x* $\overline{\qquad\qquad}$
(1)   (7)

12. device to milk the
audience

$$\overline{\quad(1)\quad}\ \overline{x}\ \overline{\quad(3)\quad}$$

13. break in affection

$$\overline{x}\ \overline{\quad(3)\quad}$$

46. SMALL TALK

Each of the words in the left-hand column has to do with the way we speak. Can you find its closest synonym in the right-hand column?

1. prattle	a. nicety
2. monologuist	b. unintelligible
3. disavow	c. hint
4. mimic	d. oration
5. profess	e. palaver
6. noncommittal	f. soliloquist
7. gaffe	g. imitate
8. incoherent	h. intelligible
9. innuendo	i. unyielding
10. gibe	j. witticism
11. dissuade	k. conversational
12. euphemism	l. excited
13. garrulous	m. deny
14. harangue	n. praise
15. admonition	o. warning
16. allegory	p. politic
17. coherent	q. parable
18. adamant	r. unconvince
19. blatant	s. blunder
20. colloquial	t. talkative
21. conjecture	u. noisy
22. boisterous	v. guess
23. accolade	w. telescoped word
24. acronym	x. allege
25. disclaimer	y. denial

47. COMMON ENTS

Hidden in each of the sentences below is the definition—as well as another clue—to a word that ends in *ent*. Can you find all the words without peeking at *Words to choose from?*

1. It isn't there now, but it may be later.
2. In transit, but producing effects that linger on.
3. This woman is wise, careful, and discreet as well.
4. I'm sensitive to sensory impressions.
5. Don't dillydally; we want a show of earnest effort.
6. The immi is so close, it's almost on us.
7. He refuses to give up on the transit system.
8. Part of the potion gives him his power.
9. The diver doesn't accept the rules.
10. Do you feel very strongly about the fur piece?
11. Dig this: insufferable poverty.
12. Not quite a cultural revolution, but a rebirth.
13. The unintentional oversight is in the ad.
14. One is sterile, the other just powerless.
15. Either or, on the scales it looks uncertain.
16. Dis person don't agree wit da group's opinion.
17. Shh! It's causing no trouble right now.
18. At the prom she's a stand-out.
19. Strictly speaking, he's at the end of his string, since circumstances have him tightly bound.
20. Her company papers don't make sense.
21. Take the train beyond the end of the line.
22. Half an omen, but add to what's already there.
23. On this part of the continent, we depend on something else happening.
24. Go around the circle to achieve a strategic victory.
25. In this state they will give you back your old job.

Words to choose from: dissident, diligent, indigent, incoherent, impotent, imminent, fervent, latent, ambivalent, inadvertent, intransigent, renascent, transient, potent, prominent, prudent, transcendent, reinstatement, quiescent, sentient, stringent, contingent, circumvent, divergent, augment.

48. MEET THE PRESS #4

Here's another set of sentences straight out of the popular press. How many make sense to you?

1. The unemployment figures are the most watched, and the most politically *potent,* of all the monthly economic reports.
   (a) troublesome (b) potential (c) powerful (d) harmful

2. Such familiar *panaceas* as public service jobs have been largely discredited.
   (a) trade-offs (b) placebos (c) cure-alls (d) rip-offs

3. The *exorbitant* cost of borrowing especially plagued the construction industry.
   (a) too-high (b) encircling (c) out of sight (d) ridiculous

4. White House officials *fervently* hope that by fall the rate will go down.
   (a) quietly (b) lately (c) slowly (d) hotly

5. Of the people lining up for hot meals, she said, "We have always had the *derelicts.*"
   (a) poor (b) bums (c) stingy (d) dirty

6. Some are *virtually* unable to work because of physical problems.
   (a) truly (b) almost completely (c) slowly (d) clearly

7. They lead a *marginal* existence or *hustle* odd jobs.
   (a) barely acceptable, work hard to get (b) doubtful, steal (c) on the outskirts, do poorly (d) edgy, scare up

8. Most discouraged workers are willing to take even the most *menial* and lowest paid jobs.
   (a) dirty (b) undignified (c) difficult (d) barren

9. The *derisive* comment was: "It was pure show business, *demeaning* the very topic it addressed."
   (a) angry, defiling (b) troublesome, muckraking (c) scornful, belittling (d) overriding, troubling

10. Predicting the size of the audience was *problematic.*
    (a) bewildering (b) difficult (c) no problem (d) impossible

11. At first she stood aloof from the planning for the *centenary,* but then she got involved.
    (a) hundredth anniversary (b) next hundred years (c) one-cent coin (d) ten-cent piece

12. The speaker *obliquely* compared Roosevelt with himself.
   (a) halfheartedly (b) confusingly (c) indirectly (d) devotedly

13. Hamilton Fish was *stigmatized* and immortalized in FDR's *lambasting* campaign refrain "Martin, Barton, and Fish."
   (a) burned, fiery (b) discredited, attacking
   (c) branded, ironic (d) singled out, tasty

14. Few of the many items of *memorabilia* were beyond repair.
   (a) mementos (b) trash (c) importance (d) worth

15. The level of radioactivity did not rise *appreciably*.
   (a) measurably (b) thankfully (c) greatly (d) truthfully

16. The mishap may be a *portent* of troubles ahead.
   (a) small taste (b) opening (c) mirror (d) warning

17. Police *cordoned off* the busy street.
   (a) put soldiers around (b) put barriers around (c) detoured
   (d) closed

18. His condition after his rescue could be described as one part shock and two parts *euphoria*.
   (a) confusion (b) numbness (c) elation (d) wisdom

19. The Italians were *jubilant* at having cracked the case.
   (a) thrilled (b) talkative (c) joyful (d) red-faced

20. *Spontaneous* cheers echoed throughout the crowd.
   (a) loud (b) sudden (c) unrehearsed (d) muted

49. DOUBLE TROUBLE

Here are definitions for 85 words, every one of which includes double letters, *ss, ll, ee, dd,* etc. They are all located horizontally in order of definition in the jumble of letters below—but beware, for there are nonsense letters between many words. And to make it a bit tougher, some of the defined words overlap.

1. a long hostile feud
2. changing boundaries to put a suburb within city limits
3. not showing a clear-cut attitude on a particular subject
4. pretend to know something
5. to produce without restraint
6. producing a strong effect
7. vulgarly flashy

8. the money lacking to meet a predetermined goal
9. an animal track
10. to avenge or repair a wrong
11. beside the point
12. pleasurable excitement
13. unattractive
14. to plan well
15. irregular or not easy to predict
16. helping to substantiate
17. fictional story that demonstrates a factual point
18. to pick and choose from a group
19. a happy escapade
20. slip fluidly through a small opening
21. not in good humor
22. to continually annoy
23. a noisy quarrel over nothing of great importance
24. effectiveness of, for instance, a sedative
25. an American technical expert in London's U.S. Embassy
26. it came from Mars, so it's called _____
27. make a bad condition somewhat better
28. unless you want to quibble, this is _____ how it is
29. chatter
30. since we disapprove of your policy, we'll _____ your next meeting
31. illegally passing a boundary line
32. to arouse sharp feelings of annoyance
33. much more than enough
34. having real-world knowhow
35. flitting along in the breeze
36. big, unpleasant, crude
37. give in
38. in a mood to start trouble
39. a Brownie point given by an admirer
40. search until you find something that's been concealed

41. to pass off a counterfeit as the real thing *(2 words)*
42. not successful at all
43. try to wreck
44. not likely to be offensive
45. wander away from the rest
46. holding down or back
47. to decide a value for taxation
48. when someone uses the wrong fork
49. someone who disagrees with an established philosophy
50. to talk somebody out of doing something
51. taking charge of somebody else's life whether they like it or not
52. the ability to just talk, talk, talk, talk, talk
53. decision to be cordial with one another
54. a sense of being of immediate importance
55. said of a person who's bad and likely to stay that way
56. when something is going to happen any day now
57. something that doesn't have the desired effect is _____
58. an implied or subtle slur on somebody's character
59. an all-out attack
60. unrealistically optimistic about everything
61. to drain of all emotional and intellectual energies
62. had as a condition since birth
63. to zig and zag out of control
64. what it is when you grab something before others can get it
65. publicity exaggeration
66. thinking about other things
67. this person held the job just before you
68. enough to see or measure
69. satisfy him so he'll keep quiet
70. hostile
71. informal kind of talk
72. a quick and big growth
73. almost without exception
74. a lack of responsibility

75. 1000 years
76. sticking one's nose in where not wanted
77. got no respect
78. senile or foolish
79. ask questions formally and systematically
80. perfect, or mighty close to it
81. not capable of being broken up
82. praise from an official
83. get rid of entirely
84. recognized as having come from someone in particular
85. tell the difference between two things

```
RAQUVENDETTANNEXATIONONONCOMMITTALXUYGHIPROFESSPULLULATELLINGI
SEDARAFFISHORTFALLINGEDSESSELLMANELLESSNNENNEINGSSPOOREDRESS
SSSEEIRRELEVANTITILLATIONALLLINNQZWIZOWANNUNPREPOSSESSINGING
INGRENGINEERRATICOLLATERALLEGORYCULLALLONNIMLYQUAZXSPREELLAN
PESEEPEEVISHARASSSSSSSSSSSSSSSSSQUABBLEFFICACYYYYYALATTACHEDEE
REXTRATERRESTRIALLEVIATEFFECTIVELYINGGGANEOUSLYEIIEPRATTLEBE
ENACIONBOYCOTTRANSGRESSIONETTLEXCESSIVELYINGIILLLSONSAVVYIEE
ARNGSCUDDINGROSSUCCUMBELLICOSELLIOUSLYYERACCOLADEFERRETTTELY
ELLOUSQUIENFOBOFFRUITLESSCUTTLEINNOCUOUSTRAGGLEREPRESSIVERRR
SSSSASSESSGAFFEDISSIDENTDISSUADEDOMINEERINGGARRULOUSNESSESSS
EVEVAVOVIVINGOLTTPPEOWIEPLIENMSPOOIGNNFMROOPDDJEEIOLLKLYPOOP
PRAPPROCHEMENTIMMEDIACYINIMIMMONNINCORRIGIBLEDOIIMMINENTININ
EININEFFECTUALLELLINNUENDOFFENSIVEPANGLOSSIANONDESSICATEOIII
REENEERKEEINECONGENITALLYCAREENEEMEERPREEMPTIVEEPUFFERYEEREE
UNPREPERPREOCCUPIEDERPREPERPRPREDECESSORAPPRECIABLEASSUAGEEE
LILLBELLIGERENTELLILLCOLLOQUIALLLINGROUNDSWELLVIRTUALLYLLYLL
LFECKLESSNESSSSESSISSOMILLENNIUMOFFICIOUSIRREVERENTDODDERING
GRINTERROGATEREIIMPECCABLEELLIINDISSOLUBLEEEAPPROBATIONNEERI
IAANNIHILATEEATTRIBUTABLEEDDDDIFFERENTIATEEERINGEERLLYOONNEXX
```

50. SCRAMBLED MAXIMS #4

The first and last halves of two familiar maxims are spelled out in the first letters of the words defined below. After you've figured out the maxims, you can use them as clues to the other halves, which are lurking in *Scrambled Maxims #7.* For an additional clue, we've filled in several letters.

1. deep chasm   _____
2. bewildering or doubtful   _____
3. a puzzle or mystery   _____

     n

     n

     y

4. continuous sequence or range   _____
5. continual fluctuation   _____
6. experienced secondhand   _____
7. based on experience or observation   _____
8. outward behavior   _____
9. choked, strangled   _____
10. friendly   _____
11. to free from guilt   _____
12. supporting evidence for a claim   _____
13. superficially polite and friendly   _____

     n

14. undiscriminating, rash, or indecent   _____

     n

15. balance   _____

Words to choose from: affable, abyss, ambivalence, demeanor, empirical, enigma, entitlement, indiscreet, equilibrium, problematic, spectrum, strangulated, suave, vicarious, vindicate.

51. FOURTH SPOTLIGHT

The word in our spotlight comes from German and literally means *lightning war.* It came into English during the Second World War, when it was used to describe violent surprise bombardments by massed air forces and mechanized ground forces acting in close coordination. By now it has come to mean any swift, vigorous attack. The spotlight word is spelled out with the first letters of every defined word. How quickly can you fill in all the missing words?

SPOTLIGHT WORD: _____

1. inheritor   _____
2. berate   _____
3. whole   _____
4. shock   _____
5. fanatic   _____
6. alarm   _____
7. explanation   _____
8. intrude   _____
9. elicit   _____
10. trick   _____

52. SUBSTITUTIONS #3

Choose the best meaning for the word in italics, to show that you understand the meaning of the entire sentence.

1. The leak in the roof is a *paradigm* of the problem with the house.
   (a) best example (b) last straw (c) paradox (d) little instance
2. The superpowers are trying for *parity* in the propaganda war.
   (a) first (b) paring down (c) equality (d) divisiveness
3. If the dollar doesn't stabilize, a lot of citizens will suffer *penury*.
   (a) slavery (b) peanuts (c) prison (d) poverty
4. Almost every idea that he planted was *pruned* or modified.
   (a) bitter (b) wrinkled (c) cut out (d) chopped down
5. The *ramifications* of the proposal are profound.
   (a) consequences (b) insinuations (c) deficiencies (d) wisdom

6. I don't *relish* going to that restaurant.
   (a) eat dessert (b) appreciate (c) resist (d) hanker

7. He felt a *renascence* of all their resistance.
   (a) restrengthening (b) supporting (c) dying (d) fleeing

8. Her *fundamentalist* interpretations got her in trouble with the committee.
   (a) strict-to-the-letter (b) down-and-out (c) sectarian
   (d) revivalist

9. The legislation was *sanctioned* by three previous administrations.
   (a) disapproved (b) approved (c) fought (d) wanted

10. Since that time, relations between the nations have escalated into *sanctions*.
    (a) approvals (b) disapprovals (c) actions forcing compliance
    (d) resistance actions

11. The *stolid* members of the church have their say, too.
    (a) distinguished (b) apathetic (c) caring (d) unsung

12. These are economically *stringent* times.
    (a) unwelcome (b) money-tight (c) lackadaisical (d) stringy

13. She let loose with a *telling* blow to the chest.
    (a) angry (b) babbling (c) counteractive (d) weighty

14. I'm not sure that I *grasp* the need to make reparations.
    (a) hold (b) contain (c) comprehend (d) finger

15. The agent's *chagrin* was so profound, I couldn't help but believe his story.
    (a) sorrow (b) wisdom (c) charge (d) embarrassment

16. Half the cost of schooling is *attributable* to the high cost of housing.
    (a) chargeable (b) blamable (c) down (d) included

17. She lacks a *coherent* approach toward the world.
    (a) complex (b) complete (c) decided (d) consistent

18. That option sounds more *calamitous* than the previous one.
    (a) stupid (b) slimy (c) miserable (d) wishful

19. It was a *farcical* episode, and one I'd like to forget.
    (a) ridiculously inept (b) candid (c) wistfully funny (d) staged

20. The poorness of the book review was *eclipsed* by the author's reputation.
    (a) heightened (b) lessened in importance (c) never noticed
    (d) doubled

53. TRUE OR FALSE

All the words in the left-hand column have to do with truth or falseness. Can you match them with their closest *antonyms* (opposites) in the right-hand column?

1. credible	a. promise
2. veritable	b. unjustifiably
3. authenticator	c. aboveboard
4. bogus	d. conviction
5. candor	e. brainwash
6. chicanery	f. genuine
7. crocodile	g. false
8. debrief	h. unbelievable
9. recant	i. suspect
10. rhetoric	j. sincere
11. substantive	k. prove
12. righteously	l. verifiable
13. trumped up	m. impermissibility
14. feigned	n. deceit
15. duplicitous	o. moniker
16. dubious	p. guilelessness
17. hypothetical	q. impugner
18. skepticism	r. sorrowful
19. purported	s. insubstantial
20. plausible	t. holding water
21. inequity	u. discounted
22. legitimacy	v. indisputable
23. refute	w. justice
24. pseudonym	x. denied
25. alleged	y. frankness

54. MORE FAMILY RESEMBLANCES

In each series, all but one of the words belong in the same family. Circle the word that's an outsider, and tell what the others have in common.

1. detrimental, hamper, impair, incapacitate, innocuous, toxic
2. fledgling, puerile, vernal, vintage
3. acronym, anonymity, euphemism, pseudonym
4. empirical, hypothetical, ingenuity, speculate
5. abort, deter, institute, obstructionist, preclude
6. blitzkrieg, holocaust, kamikaze, salvo
7. default, deficit, fiscal, shortfall, penury
8. boycott, foray, insurgency, offensive
9. formidable, gargantuan, grandiose, minuscule, plethora
10. catalyst, mentor, obliging, incorrigible
11. kamikaze, macabre, moribund, putative, specter
12. derisive, fandango, farcical, jest, ludicrous
13. fervent, mawkish, poignant, stolid, volatile
14. apotheosis, avatar, entrepreneur, menial, mogul
15. attaché, envoy, junta, mentor, protégé
16. fundamentalist, pacifist, pragmatist, populist, skeptic
17. harangue, mimic, monologist, palaver, rhetoric
18. chicanery, cuckold, gambit, ploy, vulpine
19. diligent, lax, meticulous, prudent
20. adulation, discipline, dissident, espouse

55. SHADES OF MEANING

The language is filled with words that have somewhat the same meaning. For each pair of words defined below, decide which means which.

1. (a) stigmatize   (1) denounce as being dangerous
   (b) proscribe   (2) mark as being contemptible
2. (a) unconscionable   (1) uncontrollable
   (b) incorrigible   (2) unreasonable
3. (a) vindicate   (1) free from blame
   (b) reinstate   (2) restore to prior position
4. (a) redress   (1) to disprove with evidence
   (b) refute   (2) to set right or make up for
5. (a) grouse   (1) complaint
   (b) grievance   (2) complaint for a reason
6. (a) nostrum   (1) ineffective cure
   (b) panacea   (2) cure for everything
7. (a) contrition   (1) a confession of error
   (b) recantation   (2) sorrow for error
8. (a) culpable   (1) guilty of wrongdoing
   (b) infamous   (2) criminal or bad
9. (a) transgression   (1) going beyond the law's limits
   (b) subversion   (2) working against the government
10. (a) inequity   (1) difference
    (b) disparity   (2) unfairness
11. (a) instigate   (1) to push forward
    (b) institute   (2) to start moving
12. (a) disavow   (1) to let go voluntarily
    (b) waive   (2) to deny responsibility for
13. (a) domineering   (1) preventing expression
    (b) repressive   (2) controlling
14. (a) shrewd   (1) tricky
    (b) spurious   (2) deceitful
15. (a) demean   (1) to corrupt
    (b) defile   (2) to lower in status
16. (a) lambaste   (1) to attack verbally
    (b) harangue   (2) to speak pretentiously
17. (a) traumatization   (1) worry

(b) trepidation　　　　　(2) emotional harm
18. (a) educe　　　　　　(1) to figure out
　　 (b) perceive　　　　 (2) to sense
19. (a) officious　　　　　(1) dominating
　　 (b) overarching　　　(2) meddling
20. (a) nurture　　　　　 (1) to encourage development
　　 (b) foster　　　　　 (2) to help development

56. MEET THE PRESS #5

Try your hand at one more set of sentences straight from the popular press.

1. They suffered years of *impotent* anguish, watching helplessly as terrorists bombed and kidnapped.
   (a) strong (b) unhelpful (c) powerless (d) defenseless

2. The Brigades *faction* decided to reassert its strength with an especially bold gesture.
   (a) crowd (b) wing (c) melange (d) junta

3. The police search managed an *unprecedented* penetration of the Red Brigades.
   (a) first-time (b) unheralded (c) uncalled-for (d) one-time

4. At home there is a bitter *polarization* between the self-interested rich and the resentful poor.
   (a) irony (b) division (c) opposition (d) wishing

5. The government is attempting to set an example of *austerity*.
   (a) simplicity (b) anguish (c) coldness (d) sterility

6. He proved to be the perfect *foil* for the dynamic Sadat: efficient, disciplined, self-effacing.
   (a) thin sheet (b) writing paper (c) contrast (d) lackey

7. She has been able to bring about a *tangible* if subtle change in the country's mood.
   (a) real (b) touching (c) constant (d) temporary

8. They've been brought up on charges of *fomenting* religious strife.

(a) *churning up* (b) *measuring* (c) *tormenting* (d) *starting up*

9. On the arms question they may ask for *parity* with Israel.
(a) *trouble* (b) *equal settlement* (c) *division*
(d) *equal buying power*

10. They don't want any *overt* concessions that would make Egypt lose *credibility* in the Arab world.
(a) *quick, responsibility* (b) *noticeable, believability*
(c) *total, respect* (d) *old, face*

11. The spokesman charged that the Kremlin was "bent on the *mortification* of national dignity."
(a) *defiance* (b) *embarrassment* (c) *humiliation* (d) *killing*

12. They seem to have learned nothing from the numerous grave *ruptures* in the past.
(a) *outbreaks* (b) *breaches of the peace* (c) *floods*
(d) *breaches in the line*

13. Many believe that the current *schism* is irreversible.
(a) *party line* (b) *witch hunt* (c) *break between people*
(d) *refusal to cooperate*

14. The image that flashed on the screen was a *veritable* bust of the great master.
(a) *close as you can get* (b) *too close for comfort* (c) *provable*
(d) *magnificent*

15. Especially noticeable were his advanced age and less than robust *demeanor*.
(a) *paunch* (b) *fury* (c) *body* (d) *behavior*

16. We expected them to use their *formidable* authority to ensure an orderly transfer of power.
(a) *total* (b) *awesome* (c) *futile* (d) *useful*

17. In the *arcane* field of Kremlinology, they are the two most important counselors.
(a) *mysterious* (b) *troubled* (c) *tricky* (d) *sugary*

18. The *exultant* guerillas quickly issued a communique claiming that they had destroyed several aircraft.
(a) *jubilant* (b) *devious* (c) *remaining* (d) *exiting*

19. The *deficit* ran to over a hundred billion dollars.
(a) *defeat* (b) *bill* (c) *loss* (d) *cost*

20. The debate in the House of Commons was *acrimonious*.
(a) *fiery* (b) *tasty* (c) *marked by harsh words*
(d) *marked by foot-stomping*

57. SCRAMBLED MAXIMS #5

Again, the first letter of every word, reading from top to bottom, spells out the halves of two old sayings. Can you spell out the maxims—and then locate the *scrambled maxim* that contains the other halves of both sayings?

1. comparison by substitution   _____
2. opposite of hidden   _____
3. quack remedy   _____
4. of suicidal air crashes   _____
5. clear and unmistakable   _____
6. second person singular or plural   _____
7. short newspaper item   _____
8. provable by seeing or doing   _____
9. arm of the sea   _____
10. luminous   _____
11. opposite of offensive or harmful   _____
12. loud warning signal   _____
13. of man's effect on environment   _____
14. jargon or code language   _____
15. to transfer property, bargain, or manage   _____
16. opposite of elect   _____
17. foolish, silly   _____
18. opposite of unskillful   _____
19. frenzy or rage, often of a group   _____
20. an attack   _____
21. a negativist or interferer   _____
22. deserved lickings, beatings   _____

Words to choose from: argot, deft, ecological, estuary, explicit, furor, empirical, innocuous, kamikaze, klaxon, ludicrous, lumps, lustrous, metaphor, negotiate, nostrum, obstructionist, offensive, overt, oust, squib, you.

58. PERSONALITIES

The language is filled with words that express personality quirks. See if you can match the quirks that appear in the left-hand list with their *antonyms* or opposites in the right-hand list.

1. a *flamboyant* dresser	a. obvious
2. an *obstructionist* when work is to be done	b. ornate
3. an *intransigent* arguer	c. imaginative
4. a *banal* sense of humor	d. resultful
5. a *bogus* ambassador	e. unfeeling
6. an *intimidating* stare	f. unostentatious
7. a *latent* cat-lover	g. pious
8. a *penchant* for green peas and honey	h. honest
9. *mawkish* about babies	i. protective
10. a *meticulous* carpenter	j. helper
11. an *austere* hairdo	k. deliberate
12. *deft* with a paintbrush	l. real
13. *precipitate* in making decisions	m. awkward
14. a *bland* way of speaking	n. yielding
15. an *irreverent* jokester	o. brusque
16. an *ingenious* designer	p. satisfiable
17. a *domineering* spouse	q. dislike
18. an *ineffectual* leader	r. submissive
19. an *insatiable* appetite	s. dull-witted
20. *duplicitous* in dealing with others	t. careless

59. NO MATTER

As you can see, *no* appears in all the words below. Read the questions and fill in the missing letters.

1. What's something you take to kill pain?   *an* <u> no   </u>

2. What's a totally inoffensive
   person?

   _____no_____

3. What's a person who talks
   nonstop?

   a _____no_____

4. What if you won't tell
   your name?

   you're _____no_____

5. What's the way you look
   and act?

   your _____no_____

6. Why won't the woman
   offer an opinion?

   she's no_____

7. What's an independent
   country?

   _____no_____

8. What's something that
   deviates from the norm?

   an ___no_____

9. What's a famous person?

   _____no_____

10. What's a medicine that
    probably doesn't help?

    a no_____

60. HOW VERBAL ARE YOU #3

Now that you've done a few verb-finding games, we'll make it a bit
tougher. How many verbs can you find from just the definitions and the
additional clues—without the crutch of words to choose from?

1. to prevent from acting (5 *letters beginning with d*)

2. to fold into twists and turns (9 *letters beginning with c*)

3. to move or speak hesitatingly; to lose effectiveness (6 *letters
   beginning with f*)

4. to bring out; to deduce (5 *letters beginning with e*)

5. to deny responsibility for something (7 *letters beginning with d*)

6. to make better by filling completely with something (6 *letters
   beginning with i*)

7. to keep from moving by using obstacles (6 *letters beginning
   with h*)

8. to speak or act without being serious (4 *letters beginning with j*)

9. to wander or wind casually along a path (*7 letters beginning with m*)

10. to come between two others (*9 letters beginning with i*)

11. to become liable for something, such as damages (*5 letters beginning with i*)

12. to sink under a weight, as if sinking under water (*7 letters beginning with f*)

13. to penetrate sufficiently enough that one understands (*6 letters beginning with f*)

14. assume an air of superiority (*10 letters beginning with c*)

15. to motivate (*7 letters beginning with i*)

16. to prod into action (*4 letters beginning with g*)

17. to devote to a purpose showing great dedication (*10 letters beginning with c*)

18. to speak badly of someone (*6 letters beginning with m*)

19. to go up in amount or intensity (*8 letters beginning with e*)

20. to make fun of through imitation (*5 letters beginning with m*)

61. A NATION OF ATIONS

The Latin ending *ion* (originally meaning "state of," "act of," or "process of") has been added to so many English verbs and adjectives ending in *ate* (with the final "e" being dropped along the way) that other words that didn't originally end in *ate* have formed their nouns with the ending *ation*. Can you name the nouns in our word list that all end in *ation*?

1. a cry of grief

2. a back and forth movement

3. movement to opposite ends of an issue

4. uncertainty mixed with some fear

5. a face-to-face clash of ideas

6. calling on someone for moral support

7. a legal battle

8. standing so long it becomes stale

9. formal approval

10. denying oneself life's luxuries

11. turning one's assets into cash

12. a systematized statement

13. a deviation from the norm or unsoundness of mind

14. a bit of something that's pleasurably exciting

15. humiliation to one's self-respect

16. a consequence of one's actions

17. extreme admiration

18. public condemnation

19. a person who's a prime example of a particular quality

20. the attachment of a new thing to an old one

Words to choose from: aberration, adulation, annexation, approbation, confrontation, denunciation, fluctuation, formulation, incarnation, invocation, lamentation, liquidation, litigation, mortification, polarization, ramification, renunciation, stagnation, titillation, trepidation.

62. CURRENT EVENTS

Test your understanding of these sentences that appeared in a newsmagazine.

1. The book is full of strange tales of grieving women and *domineering* men.
   (a) ruling (b) tyrannizing (c) fat (d) game-playing

2. There are bewildered husbands, inexplicable marriages, and *acrimonious* separations.
   (a) tearful (b) harsh-worded (c) angry (d) sanctimonious

3. The *drab* effect is of *trite* case studies masquerading as literature.
   (a) olive-green, useless (b) uninteresting, hackneyed
   (c) grubby, silly (d) brag, useless

4. It focused on the private lives laid bare by *pervasive* surveillance.
   (a) thorough (b) constant (c) obnoxious (d) long

5. Privately, he is a decent if *doddering* family man.
   (a) silly (b) fatherly (c) anything (d) talkative

6. As an *ambivalent* figurehead for Big Business, he earns little sympathy.
   (a) either-handed (b) even-handed (c) uncertain (d) valueless

7. The Chinese assumptions about the role art plays in society are *sundered* from those *postulates* we normally carry with us.
   (a) torn, posters (b) devised, ideas (c) shining, afterthoughts
   (d) completely separate, premises

8. News editors were briefed on *severance* arrangements to go into effect if the newspaper closes.
   (a) harsh (b) dismissal (c) pay (d) worship

9. Computer crime is an ongoing challenge that demands *diligent* attention.
   (a) unrelenting (b) relative (c) daily (d) weekly

10. The computer has become a source of *trepidation* as well as an indispensable tool.
    (a) timidity (b) tripping (c) rapid advances (d) worry

11. Legislation has *languished* in committee as legislators have concentrated on tax issues.
    (a) lengthened (b) run rampant (c) lain inert (d) been changed

12. Much of the *chicanery* goes undetected.
    (a) trickery (b) chicken-stealing (c) fancy talk (d) sugar cutting

13. A New York banker *pilfered* secret information from a rival bank.
    (a) filtered (b) pulled out (c) bought (d) swiped

14. The bonuses became a bitter issue during an *acrid* House of Commons debate.
    (a) ceremonious (b) bitter (c) quick (d) masterful

15. The present standoff between bankers and Poles could go on *interminably*.
    (a) indeterminately (b) from time to time (c) forever
    (d) interestingly

16. If they demand too much too soon, bankers will declare Poland *in default*, and they'll stand little chance of receiving what is owed to them.
    (a) in error (b) as having poor judgment
    (c) as losing their rights (d) at fault

17. This is a problem that will not go away no matter how much politicians *harangue and harass* the chairman.
(a) talk at and annoy (b) try and stop (c) beg and argue
(d) follow and kick

18. Intense *negotiations* began, *faltered* once, and then picked up speed.
(a) displays, stopped (b) bargains, tripped
(c) developments, halted (d) bargaining, lost steam

19. Both sides should draw *solace* from their success.
(a) praise (b) standing (c) polish (d) comfort

20. One explanation being *bruited about* is that people might have begun withdrawing their money.
(a) boasted (b) forced on people (c) whispered around
(d) told and retold

63. SHADES OF MEANING #2

Sometimes two words are so close in meaning, we use them interchangeably. Sometimes the difference in meaning is just wide enough that they can't be substituted for one another. From the choices in each set below, decide which word has which meaning.

1. (a) memorabilia   (1) based on memory
   (b) retrospective   (2) things worth remembering
2. (a) ponder   (1) to wonder about
   (b) conjecture   (2) to guess about
3. (a) excessive   (1) more than is normal
   (b) exorbitant   (2) exceeding normal limits
4. (a) evoke   (1) to bring into the open
   (b) elicit   (2) to call to mind
5. (a) diversion   (1) distracting the attention from reality or routine
   (b) escapism   (2) distracting the attention from unhappiness
6. (a) anonymous   (1) giving no name
   (b) pseudonymous   (2) giving a false name

7. (a) denunciation	(1) rejection	
(b) renunciation	(2) accusation	
8. (a) euphoric	(1) triumphant	
(b) exultant	(2) elated	
9. (a) imperative	(1) what must be done	
(b) inevitable	(2) what must happen	
10. (a) indigent	(1) stingy with money	
(b) penurious	(2) lacking life's comforts	
11. (a) broach	(1) start and carry out	
(b) mount	(2) bring up a subject	
12. (a) polarizing	(1) dividing into two opposites	
(b) divisive	(2) creating disagreement	
13. (a) grandiose	(1) splendid or exaggerated	
(b) magnific	(2) dignified or pompous	
14. (a) ostensibly	(1) apparently; not necessarily	
(b) putatively	(2) supposedly; assumably	
15. (a) hypothesis	(1) guesswork on slight grounds	
(b) conjecture	(2) supposition without any proof	
16. (a) explicit	(1) visible without any vagueness	
(b) overt	(2) completely open to view	
17. (a) plausible	(1) observable	
(b) empirical	(2) reasonable	
18. (a) evasive	(1) avoiding direct response	
(b) elusive	(2) avoiding direct grasp	
19. (a) gyrate	(1) turn round and round	
(b) careen	(2) move from side to side	
20. (a) avidly	(1) strongly opposed	
(b) adamantly	(2) strongly eager	

64. SOME MORE PERSONALITIES

Here are some more words that express personality quirks. Match those that appear in the left-hand column with their *antonyms* or opposites in the right-hand list.

1. an *unprepossessing* style of dress
2. a *simplistic* attitude toward world affairs
3. *spontaneous* charm
4. *spunky* on the football field
5. *savvy* about many topics
6. *polymathic* when it comes to ancient history
7. a *puerile* sense of humor
8. *erratic* behavior toward others
9. *obliging* when favors are requested
10. given to *laconic* statements
11. *divisive* among acquaintances
12. an *incorrigible* taste for warm beer
13. an *insouciant* lack of enthusiasm
14. a *feckless* swinger on the tennis courts
15. *elusive* when needed most
16. *ingratiating* toward elders
17. *inept* with a kitchen knife
18. stands by *impotently*
19. works in a *desultory* manner
20. goes at a job *mercurially*

a. cowardly
b. effective
c. mature
d. long-winded
e. skillful
f. concerned

g. overcomplicating
h. unifying
i. rehearsed
j. dispensing
k. accessible
l. ignorant
m. empty-headed
n. resolutely
o. inconsiderate
p. powerfully
q. consistent
r. attractive
s. reformable
t. methodical

65. EUPHEMISMS

We all have our ups and downs, and some of our moods are more attractive than others. We can magically make a less attractive mood appear more attractive if we know the *euphemism* for it: the more agreeable sounding word that means the same thing. From the list on the right, find a euphemism for each expression on the left.

1. mawkish	a. ironic
2. reckless	b. litigious
3. bossy	c. audacious
4. argumentative	d. intrusive
5. lazy	e. banal
6. ridiculous	f. vacuous
7. narrow-minded	g. intimidating
8. threatening	h. conciliatory
9. sarcastic	i. officious
10. cure-all	j. mercurial
11. embittered	k. arbitrary
12. empty-headed	l. avid
13. greedy	m. acrid
14. interfering	n. irreverent
15. contrary	o. mordant
16. moody	p. macabre
17. appeasing	q. panacea
18. ordinary	r. ludicrous
19. disappointed	s. flamboyant
20. insensitive	t. sentimental
21. weird	u. perverse
22. meddlesome	v. stolid
23. disrespectful	w. languorous
24. flashy	x. chagrined
25. sarcastic	y. parochial

66. MAKE-A-WORD #3

The letters of the highlighted word appear, in order, where we've put an *x* in each word defined below. Using the definitions and numbers of letters as clues, how fast can you fill in the highlighted word and use it to find the rest of the words? (Note: continues on next page.)

_____ (a word meaning *unattractive* or *uninfluential*)

1. showing no current activity

$\overline{}_{(1)}$ $\overline{x}$ $\overline{}_{(7)}$

2. excessively

$\overline{}_{(1)}$ $\overline{x}$ $\overline{}_{(4)}$

3. break apart

$\overline{}_{(2)}$ $\overline{x}$ $\overline{}_{(4)}$

4. dealing with raw emotions

$\overline{}_{(5)}$ $\overline{x}$ $\overline{}_{(2)}$

5. a separately existing thing

$\overline{x}$ $\overline{}_{(5)}$

6. rumored

$\overline{}_{(3)}$ $\overline{x}$ $\overline{}_{(5)}$

7. explosively changeable

$\overline{}_{(1)}$ $\overline{x}$ $\overline{}_{(6)}$

8. a break between people

$\overline{}_{(4)}$ $\overline{x}$ $\overline{}_{(1)}$

9. a tribute of gunshots

$\overline{x}$ $\overline{}_{(4)}$

10. well-fed

$\overline{}_{(4)}$ $\overline{x}$ $\overline{}_{(2)}$

11. itemized list

$$\overline{}_{(2)} \; x \; \overline{}_{(3)}$$

12. painfully or extremely

$$x \; \overline{}_{(5)}$$

13. capable of adequate development

$$\overline{}_{(1)} \; x \; \overline{}_{(4)}$$

14. complete distaste, withdrawal

$$\overline{}_{(8)} \; x$$

15. sink lower in condition

$$\overline{}_{(2)} \; x \; \overline{}_{(7)}$$

67. X MARKS THE SPOT CROSSWORD

All the words defined in this puzzle have an *x* in them.

Across

1. from somewhere other than the earth
2. to project an unknown number by using knowns: extra – – – – – –
3. it seems contradictory
5. to be full of joy
6. to clear of wrongdoing
8. a case of expanding too far: – – – – extension
9. taking on too much: over – – – – – – – –
13. a flowing in
14. not strict
16. poisonous
17. manuscript surroundings

18. model a behavior for others to follow
19. long rows of closely marching troops
20. not what it seems to be

Down

1. take what belongs to someone else
4. take on more than you can handle: – – – – extend
5. show for others to follow
7. adding one entity to another
10. to demand
11. a warning horn
12. the way in which words are formed into sentences
15. poisoning

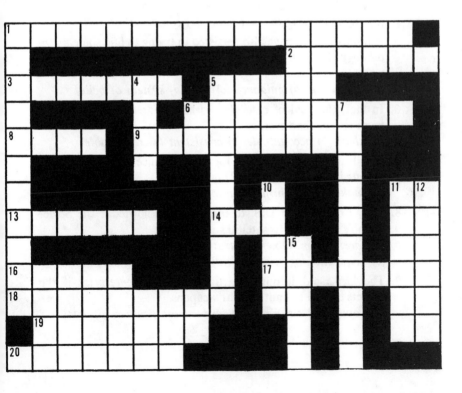

68. MEET THE PRESS #6

Once again, we've found one short news article in the popular press that contains many words we've chosen to highlight. Does the writer know more words than you?

1. The catchword "linkage" has *profound* appeal for any American who *ponders* the dilemma of having to share the planet with the U.S.S.R.
   (a) strong, discusses (b) proven, confronts (c) terrible, hits on (d) deep, weighs

2. Soviet internal and foreign policies are *anathema* to American interests.
   (a) a curse (b) opposite (c) destructive (d) chargeable

3. The accumulation of dangerous weaponry makes it *imperative* that they try to get along.
   (a) important (b) necessary (c) a wish (d) a difficulty

4. Even the most *righteously* anti-Soviet Secretaries of State always pick up where their predecessors left off.
   (a) right-thinking (b) justifiably (c) conservatively (d) truly

5. Administrations have also persisted in trying to find some *methodology* that will make it harder for the Soviets to have their way.
   (a) procedure (b) guidance (c) way (d) system of belief

6. In fact, the goal of *credible*, workable agreement now seems more elusive than ever.
   (a) clear (b) accountable (c) consistent (d) reasonable

7. The leadership was eager for a conference that would *consecrate* its post-World War II borders.
   (a) make sacred (b) firm up (c) construct (d) corner

8. They expected the U.S. to *implicitly* acknowledge the Soviet Union's *sway* over its satellites.
   (a) carefully, movement (b) truthfully, domination
   (c) unquestioningly, control (d) without saying so, rule

9. The U.S. said it might participate in the *enterprise* if the Soviets agreed to limit nuclear weapons.
   (a) voyage (b) risky project (c) business acumen (d) war

10. He retorted that Congress would *impose punitive sanctions.*
    (a) compel laws aimed at punishing (b) force silly reprisals
    (c) put aside existing measures (d) destroy deceptive practices

11. It was transformed into a *rationale* for punishing the Soviets.
    (a) explanation (b) diversion (c) ratio (d) retaliation

12. The Soviets, meanwhile, saw their partner in *detente* politically *incapacitated.*
    (a) the teeth, uninvolved (b) close quarters, defeated
    (c) truth, involved (d) eased relations, disabled

13. Pressure from American farmers led to the lifting of the grain *embargo.*
    (a) fleet (b) trade ban (c) working agreement (d) defeat

14. Pressure from *pragmatists* led to renewed negotiations.
    (a) practical people (b) numbers runners (c) numismatists
    (d) stuffed shirts

15. The talks continued despite the *imposition* of *martial* law in the satellite.
    (a) taking, arbitrary (b) hardship, Greek (c) infliction, military
    (d) posting, arbitrary

16. It was designed to be a *vehicle* for altering Soviet behavior.
    (a) passageway (b) transport (c) device (d) formula

17. The gesture was *gratuitous,* and hardly even a slap on the wrist.
    (a) uncalled-for (b) graceful (c) ungracious (d) graceless

18. The lack of communication tends to point up the absence of a *cohesive* long-range policy.
    (a) consistent (b) understandable (c) band-aid (d) temporary

19. There is every indication of the *eventuality* that meetings will take place.
    (a) time (b) possible outcome (c) definite plan (d) hope

20. We expect a *furor* if the agreement isn't *ratified.*
    (a) madness, explained (b) disagreement, agreed on
    (c) public uproar, okayed (d) turmoil, signed

69. SCRAMBLED MAXIMS #6

The first and last halves of two familiar sayings are spelled out in the first letters of the words defined below. Elsewhere among our *Scrambled Maxims* are the missing halves. We've started you off with two letters. Try not to peek at *Words to choose from* until you're done.

1. to make unclean, impure, or corrupted _____
2. opposite of straightforwardly _____
3. offering no opinion _____
4. Russian threesome _____
5. old joke or platitude _____
6. opposite of unrelated _____

         y

7. opposite of faulty or blameworthy _____

         n

8. changeableness or impermanence _____
9. opposite of cooperate with _____
10. study of life in its surroundings _____

11. lesson book _____
12. never-before, wonderful, extraordinary _____
13. in foreign policy, easing of tension _____
14. follower or idea spreader _____
15. quality of being important at this moment _____
16. to prick or annoy _____
17. injustice or complaint _____

Words to choose from: chestnut, detente, disciple, defile, ecology, hamper, impeccable, immediacy, grievance, nettle, noncommittal, obliquely, relevant, primer, transience, troika, unprecedented.

70. IT'S ABOUT TIME

All the words in the left-hand column have to do with time or its use. Match the following words with their *antonyms* (opposites) in the right-hand column.

1. inevitable		a.	irregular
2. sporadic		b.	certainty
3. terminate		c.	deliberate
4. transience		d.	begin
5. dilatory		e.	late
6. precipitate		f.	permanence
7. chronic		g.	frequent
8. eventuality		h.	early
9. millennium		i.	uncertain
10. matinal		j.	Armageddon

Match the following words with their *synonyms* in the right-hand column.

11. portent		k.	immediate
12. predecessor		l.	negligent
13. interim		m.	recess
14. interminably		n.	innate
15. imminent		o.	forerunner
16. derelict		p.	forever
17. moratorium		q.	concurrent
18. simultaneously		r.	forecast
19. outmoded		s.	waiting time
20. congenital		t.	obsolete

71. FAMILY RESEMBLANCES #3

In each series, all but one of the words belong in the same family. Circle the word that's an outsider, and tell what the others have in common.

1. altruistic, antagonize, harass, litigious, martial
2. ingratiating, lambaste, negotiate, rapprochement
3. insouciant, raffish, suave, urbane
4. crudity, euphemism, gaffe, scatalogical
5. acuity, epiphany, facade, fathom, grasp
6. adamant, domineering, intimidating, intransigent, shrewd
7. oligarchy, regime, triumvirate, troika
8. bifurcate, bilateral, divisive, intrusive
9. imponderable, insatiable, myriad, pullulate
10. burnished, drab, ocher, wan
11. disparity, feign, fob off, simulate, spurious
12. candor, hypothetical, integral, substantive, veritable
13. bumbling, ineffectual, ineptitude, perfunctory, sleazy
14. junta, phalanx, protégé, retinue, troika
15. enigma, ponder, speculate, trepidation
16. ominous, portent, prerequisite, presage
17. apathetic, hanker, penchant, propensity
18. cardinal, imponderable, limbo, myriad
19. abstraction, perspective, rendering, simulate
20. cull, lumps, swelter, tedious, traumatize

72. WHY Y? WHY NOT?

How many missing words can you fill in without looking at the *Words to choose from?* Here's an added clue: each word ends in *y.*

1. The words in the pamphlet were _____y.
   (inflammatory)

2. The teacher has a unique _____y for teaching children to read. *(set of procedures)*

3. During an auto race, racers often _____y for the best position. *(maneuver deviously)*

4. The _____y of the request made me stop what I was doing. *(need to be done at once)*

5. Ahab's _____y was achieved when he caught Moby Dick. *(sudden understanding of the essence of life)*

6. Her attempts at gardening are _____y at best. *(unplanned and irregular)*

7. "MacBird" was a _____y of Lyndon Johnson. *(imitation in order to ridicule)*

8. The youths went on an _____y of terror. *(uncontrolled wild action)*

9. All Hallow's Eve is a night of _____y. *(trickery)*

10. A tumor is an _____y in the body's cells. *(deviation from normal)*

11. Many kings have ruled in an _____y manner. *(random, unjust, and oppressive)*

12. Both sides have to _____y the agreement. *(formally approve)*

13. Throwing a snowball at the snowball thrower is a _____y act. *(revengeful)*

14. It was their _____y that made me decide to stop trying to teach them anything. *(lack of interest or concern)*

15. The old man celebrated his _____y. *(hundredth birthday)*

16. _____y is a fancy way of saying "effectiveness."

17. She was wearing a _____y blouse. *(shoddily made)*

18. The dog won't stop barking. He sure is _____y. *(full of spirit)*

19. An _____y of the Gulf of Mexico flows into the Mississippi. *(arm of the sea that joins a river)*

20. Those ideas show a _____y of intelligence. *(lack)*

Words to choose from: anomaly, apathy, arbitrary, centenary, chicanery, desultory, efficacy, epiphany, estuary, immediacy, incendiary, jockey, methodology, orgy, parody, ratify, retaliatory, sleazy, spunky, vacuity.

73 HOW VERBAL ARE YOU #4

In this verb-finding game, the sentences contain hidden definitions of the words along with clues to part of the spelling. How quickly can you figure them all out? (We've included *Words to choose from* below for additional help.)

1. A nurse, in part, furthers a person's development.
2. Often with bustle, he makes a great effort to get business.
3. The horse racer maneuvers cleverly for advantage.
4. At the seaside, they brace with supports.
5. The duo makes things physically worse.
6. The water spread throughout her unnaturally curly hair.
7. They write that she's condemned and ostracized as well.
8. The people rush en masse on a mailed letter.
9. The old bag is being dismissed without delay.
10. She knows how to read, but the point is being obscured and all trace removed.
11. Watch the wise man to get a warning of the event.
12. Half of the swelling is suffering from the heat.
13. At the pool, we think things over quietly and thoughtfully.
14. Henry, for short, has a strong and persistent desire.
15. The limper gave a grief-stricken cry.
16. From the underwater vessel, for short, we work from within to overthrow the government.
17. After part of the stabbing, all fluctuation was limited and the price held steady.
18. Offer the sixteen-ounce idea for consideration.
19. With theft in our midst, let's make a penetrating investigation.
20. Little by little, they steadily stole most of the pill.

Words to choose from: hanker, hustle, impair, jockey, lament, nurture, obliterate, permeate, ponder, presage, pilfer, probe, propound, proscribe, sack, stampede, shore up, stabilize, subvert, swelter.

74. CAT'S PLAY

Each of these tricky words has a *cat* lurking somewhere within. How many can you find from the clues we give?

1. This cat is given to obscenities   __cat_____al
2. This cat speaks with authority   ex cat_____
3. This cat is shriveled up   _____cated
4. This cat proves the mouse's genuineness   a_____cator
5. This cat's tunnel branches into two rooms   b_____cat__s
6. This cat says the prayer at the meeting   _____cation
7. This cat has stimulating ideas   p_____cat__ve
8. This cat's remarks are harsh and critical   __cat_____ng
9. This cat remains remote while causing reactions in others   cat_____ic
10. This cat's innocence is proven   _____cated

75. SUBSTITUTIONS #4

Choose the best meaning for each word in italics.

1. The executive was fired for being *dilatory*.
   (a) dreamy (b) dawdling (c) a poor worker (d) superficial
2. Her work is *replete* with errors.
   (a) complete (b) riddled (c) filled (d) depleted
3. There have been *internecine* disputes among the *troika* of top presidential advisors.
   (a) furious, array (b) time to time, dance (c) hidden, truckload (d) within the group, threesome

4. He was the victim of a *trumped-up* treason charge.
   (a) untruthfully put together (b) lying (c) overstated
   (d) indisputable

5. The color tangerine was *ubiquitous* last year.
   (a) worn all the time (b) seen everywhere (c) ugly (d) lovely

6. The jury assumed there was an *unmitigated* intent to murder.
   (a) unconditional (b) unreformed (c) circumstantial
   (d) bloodthirsty

7. The reaction of the jury was *visceral*.
   (a) bloodthirsty (b) instinctive (c) gutsy (d) calculated

8. The Prince of Wales *waived* the privileges of rank on his last trip here.
   (a) flaunted (b) underlined (c) veered from (d) relinquished

9. No *prudent* candidate would make that pledge.
   (a) cautious (b) careless (c) shortcutting (d) hesitant

10. That company policy was *propounded* by the boss's daughter.
    (a) composed (b) proposed (c) endorsed (d) confused

11. The orchestra's performance was heightened by the sound of *muted* strings.
    (a) sweet (b) soft (c) loud (d) raucous

12. The two schools involved in the *litigation* are eligible for tax exemption.
    (a) war (b) licensing (c) legal dispute (d) law

13. The Small Business Administration helps with *initiatives* for Mom-and-Pop store owners.
    (a) start-up procedures (b) energy-saving advice
    (c) constant supervision (d) action

14. Hitler's *infamy* will live in history books.
    (a) reputation (b) disaster (c) known evilness
    (d) hidden brutality

15. They are *implacably* opposed to any other method.
    (a) stubbornly (b) unbelievably (c) wistfully (d) candidly

16. The decision to reconsider gives our opponents a propaganda *coup*.
    (a) blow (b) cold (c) sedan (d) success

17. It's *attributable* to the *perfunctory* dismissal of their best player.
    (a) characteristic, funny (b) owing, unenthusiastic
    (c) next, quick (d) allowable, sudden

18. Negotiations are often filled with empty *rhetoric*.
    (a) pompous talk (b) sincerities (c) nothings (d) edicts

19. The freehand *renderings* of Mars were exquisite.
    (a) leavings (b) photos (c) drawings (d) washes

20. His behavior showed a *quantum jump* in understanding.
    (a) light year (b) large change (c) sudden increase
    (d) leap backward

76. DOUBLE THREAT #2

The words defined below make a word chain in which the last two letters of each word are also the first two letters of the following word. How quickly can you complete the chain? To start you off, we've filled in the first and last two letters in the chain.

1. a piece of banter or ridicule   ja_____

2. plodding or unimaginative   _____

3. despair or extreme pain   _____

4. bundle   _____

5. time after disaster   _____

6. religious scholar   _____

7. abnormalities or eccentricities   _____

8. to adopt and support a cause   _____

9. physical or emotional sensitivity   _____

10. hundred-year anniversary   _____ry

77. O-O CROSSWORD

Here's a hint about the words in this puzzle: they're filled with *os*. (We've added some easy words that aren't in the book's vocabulary list. We're sure you can figure them out. But don't expect every succession of letters to make a word; we're amateur puzzle-makers and you'll have to bear with us.)

Across

1. resembling one another in some way
6. action that's very unfair
12. in pilfering, the haul
14. execute an action
15. out of style
16. mishmash
18. something used to make another seem better by contrast
19. a hammer is one
20. sound of a specter
21. feeling when something bad's ahead
22. second person
24. intricately wound or twisted
26. relating to man's changing of the environment
29. to take over a group or cause
31. to throw in a high arc
32. looking for trouble
35. acronym for standing room only
37. separate into piles
38. entity: pronoun
39. animal home
40. troika
41. signal when foundering
43. interfering: _____ficious

46. tool for divesting of muck
48. lob
50. all-embracing: _____arching
51. participants in fandangos
52. to split into opposite factions
53. one of a pedestrian's vehicles
54. stroke of luck
58. interim halt
61. exclamation giving sanction for movement
62. offer an idea for discussion
63. place neither here nor there
64. sound of a garrulous cow

Down

1. the best example to be found
2. said of a self-starter
4. pseudo butter
5. therefore
7. head movement when extremely languorous
8. done out of sudden impulse (11 letters)
9. lyric poems, including one on a Grecian urn

92

10. sign warning against transgression: _____ trespassing
11. to keep afloat
13. relating to church teachings
17. child's word for muck
23. total fiery destruction
25. loud and happy
27. encircle with a no-passing sign (2 words)
28. miscalculation
30. penurious
33. klaxon sound
34. unemotional to the point of dullness
36. civilian garb
42. bill and _____
44. excessively

45. jibbed vessel that tacks
46. track of a panther
47. male predecessor of beneficiary
49. the Wizard was a mogul here
55. formidable painter-inventor: _____nardo
56. a magnific person has one that's inflated
58. Member of Parliament, for short
59. poisonous: _____xic
60. partner of #56 Down

78. SCRAMBLED MAXIMS #7

If you've completed *Scrambled Maxim #4* (#51), you're well on your way to completing this puzzle. Below, in the first letters of the defined words, are spelled out the two missing halves of the old sayings defined in #4. For an additional clue, we've filled in several letters.

1. mixture of different elements   _____
2. bitterly harsh or terribly angry   _____
3. repetitious and uninteresting   _____
4. unconcern and indifference   _____
5. course of action   _____
6. superficial   _____
7. a strong and persistent desire   _____
8. to bring about or induce   _____
                                         n
9. ruling threesome   _____
10. forceful demand or interference   _____
11. magnificent or pompous   _____
12. delegate or representative   _____
13. to incorporate into a larger unit   _____
14. one who settles on someone else's land   _____
15. opposite of interest, emotion   _____
16. sphere of activity or knowledge   _____
17. seasonal, starting a new era   _____
                                         n
                                         n
                                         y
18. likelihood, possible outcome   _____
19. unreasonable, unjust, or dictatorial   _____
20. estrangement, break in affection   _____
                                         n
21. surface center of geological disturbance   _____
22. relaxation of strained relations   _____

79. LOOK-ALIKES #2

Here are some more sets of words that look just enough alike that they can be confused in rapid reading. Connect each word to its correct synonym.

1. (a) cataclysmic, (b) catalytic   (1) calamitous, (2) causal
2. (a) invocation,
  (b) provocation   (1) prayer,
(2) inducement
3. (a) augur, (b) augment   (1) heighten, (2) foretell
4. (a) circumspect,
  (b) circumvent   (1) prevent,
(2) cautious
5. (a) coherent, (b) cohesive   (1) sensible, (2) binding
6. (a) contentious,
  (b) contingent   (1) dependent,
(2) quarrelsome
7. (a) gross, (b) grouse   (1) glaring, (2) complain
8. (a) detritus, (b) detriment   (1) harm, (2) debris
9. (a) dubious, (b) duplicitous   (1) skeptical, (2) deceitful
10. (a) dilatory, (b) diligent   (1) dawdling, (2) persevering
11. (a) hinterland, (b) heartland   (1) boondocks, (2) midlands
12. (a) garb, (b) gibe   (1) ridicule, (2) dress
13. (a) euphemism,
  (b) euphoria   (1) contentment,
(2) affectation
14. (a) precipice, (b) precipitate   (1) peak, (2) hasten
15. (a) scud, (b) scuttle   (1) ruin, (2) gust
16. (a) interim, (b) interminable   (1) perpetual, (2) pause
17. (a) harangue, (b) harass   (1) tirade, (2) torment
18. (a) derelict, (b) derisive   (1) scornful, (2) negligent
19. (a) adulate, (b) adulterate   (1) contaminate, (2) worship
20. (a) expatriate,
  (b) extrapolate,
  (c) expropriate   (1) project,
(2) outcast,
(3) evict

80. FIFTH SPOTLIGHT

The adjective in our spotlight is shifting in meaning. It started as a Latin word that meant *made holy,* and the English word that evolved once meant simply *made valid by a binding oath.* From there it began to mean also *enforced by a formal procedure.* Then it also earned the meaning *given authoritative approval or consent.*

But then the noun form of the word took on an additional meaning: *an economic or military measure, usually adopted by several nations, to force a nation violating international law to either stop or agree to a binding judgment.* As the United Nations' interventions became more and more frequent, this word was used increasingly in the news media, and recently there's been another shift. Now the noun has, in addition to its long-held meaning, a new meaning that's almost the very opposite: *a measure designed to force a country into behaving the way you want it to.* And the adjective's new additional meaning is *forcibly penalized.*

The spotlight word is spelled out where *x* marks the spot in the defined words. How quickly can you fill in every word?

SPOTLIGHT WORD: _____

1. a disastrous experience

   _____ _ _____
   (5)   *x*   (3)

2. lack of concern or feeling

   _ _____
   x   (5)

3. insight gained from an experience

   _____ _ _
   (6)   *x* (1)

4. mud

   __ _ _
   (2) *x* (1)

5. apparently

   __ _ _____
   (2) *x*   (7)

6. center, especially of an earthquake

   __ _ _____
   (2) *x*   (6)

7. contemptuous of standards

   _____ _ __
   (6)   *x* (2)

8. existent entirety

   _ _ _____
   (1) *x* (4)

9. lie about

   ___ _
   (3) *x*

10. excessively

    __ _ _____
    (2) *x*   (3)

81. HAPPENINGS

Each of the words in the left-hand column has to do with a happening. Match it with its closest definition in the right-hand column.

1. fete	a. a small lucky event
2. orgy	b. a wild party
3. coup	c. an embarrassment
4. embargo	d. a totally destructive event
5. fluke	e. a bitter feud
6. fiasco	f. political travel
7. contretemps	g. strategic arrangement
8. ground swell	h. a struggle for superiority
9. holocaust	i. repeated raids
10. insurgency	j. an elaborate party
11. scenario	k. a ban on commerce
12. vendetta	l. a brilliant success
13. ouster	m. a quickly growing event
14. stampede	n. a synopsis of projected events
15. stumping	o. a total failure
16. symposium	p. a tiny revolution
17. boycott	q. a rush of people acting together
18. deployment	r. a group refusal
19. sacking	s. a meeting
20. purge	t. a removal from authority
21. strife	u. a ridding of the opposition
22. tack	v. a brief trip outside one's territory
23. harassment	w. an attack
24. offensive	x. a quick dismissal
25. foray	y. a course of action

82. BACK PROBLEMS

The prefix *re* means "back," "backward," or "again" in many words that come from Latin. All the words defined below begin with *re*. How quickly can you find them?

1. to take back a statement or belief
2. to put back in a previous position or state
3. to put back in a former condition
4. to take back or deny the accuracy or truth of something
5. drawing back in complete distaste of something
6. giving up (drawing back from) things that please one
7. being born again
8. to say again and again
9. to leave behind (in back of) oneself
10. looking backward at things in the past
11. relating to things left behind
12. to ask, especially in writing, to get something back
13. to bring back to life or consciousness
14. to put back in its rightful condition; to get back at someone for a wrongdoing
15. getting back at someone; returning in kind
16. having one's name recognized again and again
17. acting to hold back by force
18. to reject (give back) as untrue or unjust

Words to choose from: resuscitate, repudiate, renunciation, reiterate, relinquish, revulsion, refute, recant, retrospective, renown, retaliatory, requisition, residual, renascence, reinstate, repressive, reconstitute, redress.

83. WORD TWINS #2

Here are some more sets of words that mean exactly, or nearly exactly, the same thing. How many can you fill in? (Scan the Mini-Dictionary if you get stuck.)

1. Hidden possibility   l_____
   Natural tendency   p_____
2. Weariness of mind or body   l_____
   Lack of power or vigor   i_____
3. Prevent from acting   d_____
   Prevent with obstacles from acting   h_____
4. Obscured   e_____
   Obscured or made unrecognizable   o_____
5. To collect a small tax   t_____
   The collection of money   l_____
6. A refusal of rights   d_____
   A refusal to acknowledge   r_____
7. Marked by delay   d_____
   Marked by irregularity   d_____
8. To sell something deceptively   h_____
   To deal deceptively with someone   j_____
9. Enjoying disagreements   c_____
   Creating disagreements   d_____
10. Hostile manner   a_____
    Hostile words or manner   a_____
11. Reject   r_____
    Reject as untrue   r_____
12. Two words for a spirit in   a_____
    earthly form   i_____
13. To prevent from use   p_____
    To prevent from happening   p_____
14. Old and still important   v_____
    Old and no longer used   o_____

15. Differing from one another   d _____
     Creating difference of opinion   d _____
16. Limited in range   p _____
     At the lower limit   m _____
17. To use for one's own advantage   e _____
     To control or change for one's own
     advantage   m _____
18. Disappointed or embarrassed   c _____
     Confused or embarrassed   d _____
     Embarrassed to the point of humiliation   m _____
19. A unique happening   u _____
     Unique or highly significant   e _____
20. A mixture of different elements   a _____
     A mixture of unrelated things   h _____

84. WORD WORK-OUT

This little work-out concentrates on words that are found most frequently in the working world, where some of the original meanings have been slightly shifted or refined. Ready for a bit of work? Then let's see how quickly you can find the matching definition of each work-word in the left-hand column.

1. acquisitor	a.	nonpayment
2. ante	b.	business loan
3. aspirant	c.	pay up
4. beneficiary	d.	difference in totals
5. collateral	e.	government ban on transport
6. default	f.	supporting papers
7. disparity	g.	security for debt payment
8. disclaimer	h.	surrender of legal claim
9. embargo	i.	turn to economic advantage
10. entitlement	j.	donee of valuable goods

11. exploit	k. position seeker
12. enterprise	l. business
13. entrepreneur	m. inappropriately high-priced
14. exorbitant	n. complaint
15. fiscal	o. willed gift
16. fluctuation	p. equality in buying power
17. grievance	q. monetary
18. hustle	r. price unsteadiness
19. hokum	s. business owner
20. internecine	t. great business drive
21. jurisdiction	u. response-getter
22. legacy	v. limits of authority
23. litigious	w. delay in debt payment
24. mogul	x. relating to infighting
25. moratorium	y. great failure
26. parity	z. job loss
27. severance	aa. prone to sue
28. shortfall	bb. business insufficiency
29. stabilize	cc. top man
30. tithe	dd. set a bottom price
31. indigent	ee. impasse
32. levy	ff. poverty stricken
33. deficit	gg. tax
34. fiasco	hh. receiver named in will
35. logjam	ii. money collected

85. 4-D CROSSWORD

The words defined in this puzzle begin at the numbered squares, but they continue in up to 4 different directions. We've used compass or map directions to point out the direction in which each word runs: e means to the right (east on a map), se means diagonally to the lower right, nw means diagonally to the upper left, and so on. (We've included a compass to help steer you straight.)

1 e. get rid of quickly

1 s. get rid of, as by sinking

2 e. harsh and bitter

2 se. a wild binge

2 s. of someone who's dull and emotionless: _ _ _ _ _ d

2 sw. very short *(5 letters)*

3 e. extremely self-satisfied

3 se. add this to t and get a splashing sound

3 s. an animal leaves this behind *(5 letters)*

3 sw. power over someone *(4 letters)*

4 e. tie string onto this and become very strict

5 e. hold steady

5 se. give these 4 letters to ma and make her feel ashamed

5 s. wander off course

6 e. several formal meetings to hear several experts

6 se. plan for actions

6 sw. goodies for having won

7 e. this will haunt you

7 se. this one's cheap

7 s. do this to increase the power

8 s. wed to this and you'll be biased

8 sw. the way words are supposed to be put together

9 s. smooth and polished—as a person

9 sw. not smooth and polished—as a person

10 e. put this on an ace and be comforted

10 s. if this has a tic, it looks simpler than it really is

10 se. knock apart violently *(6 letters)*

10 sw. tricky

11 e. drain off energy *(3 letters)*

11 s. fire

11 sw. flow through tiny openings

12 e. spirited

13 e. sometimes funny, sometimes sad

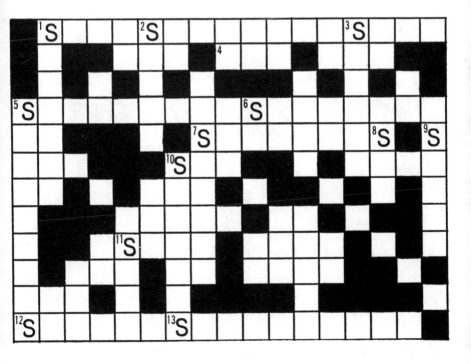

86. SCRAMBLED MAXIMS #8

You've done seven *Scrambled Maxims*, so completing this one should be a cinch. We've given you 2 letters to start off. When you're done, you should be able to put together all eight maxims in the book.

1. to exceed or outdo   _____
2. to lecture or rant at   _____
3. to dispossess or take for one's own   _____
4. lost in thought   _____
5. government in power, period of rule   _____
6. mud-yellow   _____
7. meddlesome   _____
8. surface, especially front surface   _____
9. habituated   _____
10. deviously or secretly rebellious   _____
11. meeting or compilation on a topic   _____
12. claimed or admitted   _____
13. accusation or implication   _____
14. to put before an authority   _____
15. opposite of insubstantial   _____
16. to climb or start and carry out   _____
17. questioning   _____

l

k

87. MEET THE PRESS #7

How many of these sentences, taken straight from the pages of a magazine, would you read right through without really understanding them?

1. The candidate of the far right was *purged* from the army by the new government.
(a) fired (b) exported (c) evicted (d) hired

2. Washington was seeking to *shore up* the beleaguered forces of moderation.
   (a) whitewash (b) bolster (c) advance (d) trouble

3. Since the insurgents seized power, *sporadic* fighting is an almost daily occurrence.
   (a) sputtering (b) flowery (c) trumped-up (d) off and on

4. They've been *squatting* as refugees in the mansion once belonging to the town's wealthiest man.
   (a) occupying without paying rent (b) crouching (c) hiding
   (d) using the facilities

5. Since several of them have been killed, they have good reason for their *circumspection*.
   (a) being overlooked (b) being careful (c) being roundabout
   (d) having inspection

6. They have settled village grudges through *denunciation* of their rivals.
   (a) public accusation (b) public rejection
   (c) private name-calling (d) harm

7. The West Bank *municipality* of El-Bireh has an Arab mayor.
   (a) country (b) party (c) town (d) opposition

8. The document bore the *ominous* news that the council members were all fired.
   (a) foreboding (d) disastrous (c) heavy (d) evil

9. They wore *flamboyant* berets with their *ocher* uniforms.
   (a) flaming, khaki (b) happy-looking, brown
   (c) ornate, mud-colored (d) dressy, muddy

10. Even though the bombing completely *obliterated* some areas, hopes for a quick settlement were *unduly* optimistic.
    (a) leveled, truly (b) obligated, not yet
    (c) destroyed the books, not fully (d) erased, too

11. Hama is well known as a *bastion* of the Muslim Brotherhood.
    (a) hideout (b) stronghold (c) territory (d) illegitimate child

12. All Britain was asking questions as the *enigmatic* treasure hunt continued.
    (a) dull (b) wonderful (c) hard to figure out
    (d) keeps shifting sides

13. The code-breaker was *evasive*, but the press discovered that he had taken a shrewd *tack*.
    (a) feisty, stand (b) tricky, nail (c) hesitant, position
    (d) secretive, move

14. He spent three *fruitless* nights digging around the tree.
   (a) unsuccessful (b) useless (c) hungry (d) wishful

15. The spelling and *syntax* of his letters suggest that he is not a university man.
   (a) word order (b) grammar (c) punctuation (d) handwriting

16. The current recession has gathered *momentum*.
   (a) speed (b) distance (c) acceleration (d) motive

17. If the members *curtail* output, OPEC will be *sorely* tempted to increase prices.
   (a) hurt, terribly (b) cut, badly (c) increase, truly
   (d) decrease, extremely

18. The government has *imposed* controls on more than a hundred items, and has closed down businesses that are not *complying*.
   (a) forced, obeying (b) set, withstanding (c) established, working (d) suggested, successful

19. Readers may quarrel with his *Panglossian* assessment that "we're bound to end up way ahead of where we were before."
   (a) lovable (b) simplistic (c) carefree (d) bright

20. What is more *poignant* than a bird with a lame wing, especially if he was once Rookie of the Year?
   (a) sorrowful (b) painful (c) troublesome (d) silly

88. WORDS OF ONE SYLLABLE

Words of one syllable often pack a lot of meaning. Do you know the word for each meaning—without referring to *Words to choose from?*

1. His speech was a _____ at the presidents' private lives. *(poking fun in order to amuse)*

2. That company is very _____ about rules of dress. *(the opposite of rigid)*

3. If they don't _____ the subject, I won't. *(open for discussion)*

4. Your attitude toward the war is quite _____. *(showing no personal concern)*

5. The tire can be exchanged if you have some _____ with the dealer. *(influence)*

6. _____ enjoyment if you're bored. *(pretend)*

7. It was a _____ that I won that contest. *(stroke of luck)*

8. He has a good _____ of the situation. *(understanding)*

9. To get the committee to act, use a _____. *(something that forces into action)*

10. The counselor _____ the reason for the student's rejection. *(investigated carefully)*

11. _____ your complaint in the office next door. *(put before the correct authorities)*

12. If I do something wrong, I expect to take my _____. *(deserved penalty)*

13. Did you see the _____ in the newspaper? *(short item)*

14. These are the _____ of war. *(things gained by special effort)*

15. We won't _____ for that candidate again. *(travel around showing support)*

16. The best _____ is usually the most obvious one. *(course of action)*

17. Did you see the _____ in the woods? *(wild animal's track)*

18. It fell with a _____. *(splattering sound)*

19. That's a very large _____ of papers. *(bundle)*

20. Beware; the salesman is very _____. *(clever and tricky)*

21. I've got to _____ off some fat before I can get into those clothes. *(cut away what isn't wanted)*

22. Ostrich-feathered boas once had their _____. *(period of being in fashion)*

23. Watch the athletes _____ for the crown. *(battle for superiority)*

24. For now, I'm going to ＿＿＿＿＿＿＿ the right to a hearing. *(postpone consideration of)*

25. The battle was ＿＿＿＿＿＿＿ for a hundred years. *(carried on)*

Words to choose from: spoor, squib, lumps, splat, vie, probed, clout, fluke, spoils, grasp, prune, waged, feign, lax, waive, shrewd, stump, goad, broach, jape, tack, lodge, bland, sheaf, vogue.

89. SIXTH SPOTLIGHT

Our final spotlight falls on a little word with lots of meaning—in fact, two meanings that are nearly the exact opposite of one another. The first meaning of this twentieth-century word is *to question in order to obtain useful information.* But because of the political use of the word, it has also come to mean *to instruct to reveal no classified information after release from a sensitive position.* When you hear of a person being given this treatment, which treatment is it? That's usually for the agency releasing the information to know and for you to guess at!

We do promise that the *x*s spell out our spotlighted word.

SPOTLIGHT WORD: ＿＿＿＿＿＿＿

1. occurring from time to time
   ＿＿＿＿＿ ＿ ＿＿
   (5) *x* *(2)*

2. spring-like; fresh and new
   ＿ ＿ ＿＿＿
   (1) *x* *(4)*

3. intellectual or emotional balance
   ＿＿＿＿＿＿ ＿ ＿＿＿
   (6) *x* *(4)*

4. radiant
   ＿＿＿＿ ＿ ＿＿＿
   (4) *x* *(3)*

5. look aggressive
   ＿＿ ＿ ＿＿＿
   (2) *x* *(4)*

6. support or boost
   ＿＿＿＿＿ ＿ ＿
   (5) *x* *(1)*

7. period after a destructive event
   ＿ ＿ ＿＿＿＿＿＿＿
   (1) *x* *(7)*

90. SOME MORE EUPHEMISMS

English is filled with words that say what you want to say while softening the blow a bit. Such a word is called a *euphemism,* a word that literally means "good-sounding speech." From the list on the right, find the euphemism for the expression on the left.

1. trumped-up	a. admonish
2. childish	b. culpable
3. smug	c. adamant
4. sweat	d. zealous
5. boring	e. volatile
6. rigid	f. utopian
7. punishing	g. vulpine
8. guilty	h. mediocre
9. scold	i. meticulous
10. flighty	j. unconscionable
11. rebellion	k. adulterated
12. shameless	l. tithe
13. cunning	m. tedious
14. die	n. swelter
15. picky	o. subversion
16. second-rate	p. succumb
17. diluted	q. miniscule
18. tax	r. simplistic
19. pie-in-the-sky	s. schism
20. fanatic	t. relinquish
21. falling-out	u. palaver
22. oversimplified	v. punitive
23. gab	w. puerile
24. tiny	x. fabricated
25. give up	y. complacent

91. DOUBLE-TAKES CROSSWORD

We call this crossword puzzle *Double-takes* because many of the defined words have double letters. Does that clue help? We hope so.

Across

1. to absorb into the mind or a group
4. to admit freely or claim to know
7. deer track
8. believer that we're living in a utopia
12. flattering publicity
14. excessive
15. rush of happy activity
16. contend
17. plan with skill
20. almost completely
21. loan payback reinforcement
22. showing poor judgment in conduct
23. very large
24. describes a puerile person
26. pale
27. how a toxic substance makes one feel
28. difference between what you have and what you need
30. ill-tempered or obstinate
31. broad, deep ocean wave
32. too
36. give in to great force or great desire

39. attack: _____ensive
41. golf ball holder
42. chimney liner
45. quiet or satisfy
47. unattractive, unassuming
48. boundary violation
49. opposite of mammoth

Down

1. measurable
2. one may be proscribed for committing this
3. troika
4. short for photographic simulations
6. validating procedure: sancti____
9. debrief: slang
10. intransigent: made of _____
11. what one says when one makes a gaffe
13. unsuccessful
18. answer from obstructionist
19. luster
25. entrepreneur
26. to carry out
29. a conciliatory person tries to _____d
33. to take over

34. increased in power:
    _____uped-up

35. first word in formulation of
    a hypothesis

37. bigwig

38. insect with a telling sting

40. mammoth vernal budder

41. lob

42. end product of calculation

43. outcome: ramificati_____

44. to absorb as nourishment:
    _____imilate

46. international signal of
    adversity

92. HOW VERBAL ARE YOU #5

The words that are missing from the sentences below are all verbs that contain *er* or *re*. How quickly can you fill in the blanks without referring to *Words to choose from*?

1. Fire raged, _____ everything in
   its path.   _____er_____

2. Just smell the flowers and you will
   _____ their beauty.   _____er_____

3. With long experiment, the scientist
   _____the time-honored theory.   re_____

4. The fumes _____ every corner of
   the room.   _____er_____

5. Let's _____ at Antoine's this
   evening.   re_____

6. The speaker _____ her remarks
   so that she wouldn't shock the
   audience.   _____er_____

7. I _____ the opportunity to meet
   her tomorrow.   re_____

8. My having to be there _____
   my attending the other reception.   _____re_____

9. His employment was _____ on a
   Monday.   _____er_____

10. In throwing out the unjust law, the
    judges _____ it.   re_____

11. The uneasy peace was _____ by
    gunfire.   _____re_____

12. The soldiers had to _____ the
    territory they'd won.   re_____

13. Don't _____ beyond my property
    line.   _____re_____

14. Until she was _____, I was sure
    she was dead.   re_____

15. The karate chop _____ the piece
    of wood into two halves.   _____ere_____

16. If you need paper clips, you must
_____ them on that slip of
paper.   re_____

17. Sun and rain _____ the growth
of plants.   _____er

18. I am _____ to the weight of my
glasses on my nose.   _____re_____

19. If I've said those words once, I've
_____ them a hundred times.   re_____er_____

20. The dog's chain _____ his
running.   _____er_____

Words to choose from: foster, hampers, inured, incinerating, moderated, perceive, pervaded, precludes, refuted, relish, relinquish, repudiated, requisition, reiterated, ruptured, rendezvous, resuscitated, sundered, terminate, transgress.

93. IT'S PERSONAL #2

Name the one word that sums up each of the people described below.

1. someone whose moral standards are below what's acceptable
2. someone who foretells events using omens
3. said of someone who feels elated
4. someone who takes a strong stand in a controversy
5. someone who is the epitome of a certain quality
6. a visible ghost
7. someone who's a typical example
8. said of a person who lacks the power to act
9. a person who cares about the welfare of others
10. a specialist in religious study
11. said of someone who can't make up his mind
12. an impractical idealist
13. said of a self-starter

14. a believer in the rights of the common people
15. someone who serves as a motivating influence
16. a believer in practical approaches
17. someone who comes in as a third party, especially in legal proceedings
18. someone who monopolizes the conversation
19. a taunter or joke-teller
20. a member of a governing clique

Words to choose from: activist, altruist, ambivalent, augur, autonomous, degenerate, euphoric, impotent, incarnation, inspiration, intervenor, jester, monologist, oligarch, paradigm, populist, pragmatist, specter, theologian, utopian.

94. WORDS, WORDS, WORDS

The following words all describe words. We've added some clues to help you figure them out.

1. a word formed from the first letters of many words   a____n____m
2. words that tell the truth through symbolic characters   a____g____y
3. the words surrounding and influencing a word   ____t____t
4. words in informal speech   ____l____qu____
5. the way words form sentences   ____t____x
6. can be said of overused words   tr____
7. to quarrel with loud words   ____q____le
8. a newspaper item of few words   ____q____
9. saying words clearly   ar____ation
10. agreeable words substituted for disagreeable ones   ____mi____ms
11. words that state an idea systematically   ____lation

12. describes words that lack originality   b_____l

13. a long, pompous speech   h_____gu_____

14. to speak complaining words   _____se

15. tending to use an annoying number of words   g_____lo_____

16. using disjointed, unconnected words   _____nc_____e_____t

17. words that hint evil of a person   _____n_____o

18. word substituted for another to suggest comparison of ideas   _____or

19. words that show grief   _____e_____a_____ns

20. words that imitate   _____ry

95. END PLAY #2

Many nouns end in *ity*. Peel off the ending and you may find an adjective. But nearly as often, what you have left is just a group of nonsense syllables. Below are a number of statements that contain *ity* nouns. Mark whether each statement is true or false.

1. People who catch on quickly often have poor acuity. _____

2. In the midwest, tornadoes are a common adversity. _____

3. A sophisticated design is an example of crudity. _____

4. The parts of this book are its entity. _____

5. Next Fourth of July is an eventuality. _____

6. Albany, New York, is a municipality. _____

7. Picasso had a propensity to draw and paint. _____

8. Einstein was noted for his vacuity. _____

9. Because it's given unearned, a tip is called a gratuity. _____

10. A calamity is always something that happens to someone else. _____

11. People spend lavishly in times of austerity. _____

12. A disabled person has an incapacity. _____

13. A person who copies others' ideas has individuality. _____

14. It's your insatiability that makes you so easily satisfied. _____

15. People who become famous escape mediocrity. _____

16. The plausibility of an idea makes scientists think twice about believing it. _____

17. The spontaneity of the performance testified to the fact that it had been rehearsed. _____

18. We could grab the ghost because of its tangibility. _____

19. Its ubiquity makes green a popular color this year. _____

20. The viability of the idea assures us that it will work adequately well. _____

96. LOADED WORDS #2

Once again we'll show that you can put a great deal of meaning into one word—if you know the word. Can you find the missing word in each sentence without peeking at *Words to choose from?*

1. When it comes to deciding how to spend her salary, she's a _____. *(practical person)*

2. Color-blind people can't _____ between red and green. *(see any difference)*

3. The victim's spouse sank into an _____ of grief. *(pit too deep to measure)*

4. It doesn't pay to _____ over every exam. *(suffer agony)*

5. Television viewers often experience events _____. *(as if they were actually participating)*

6. A college degree is a _____ for most executive jobs. *(something required in advance)*

7. The child _____ when I told him to pick up his room. *(looked passively aggressive)*

8. That excuse for being late is an old _____. *(been used so often, it's stale)*

9. Whenever Elvis Presley went anywhere, his _____ came along. *(group of people who attended to his needs)*

10. The airline cancellation left my travel plans in _____. *(neither here nor there)*

11. If our plans _____, we'll meet. *(are the same)*

12. Can you see the problem from my _____? *(way of looking at things)*

13. The first thing the new president did was to _____ his cabinet. *(get rid of disloyal members)*

14. In a novel by Golding, a child emerges from a _____. *(area being completely destroyed by fire)*

15. When it comes to the law, I'm a _____. *(person who believes in strict adherence)*

16. When the astronauts touched land, they were _____ before they were permitted to do anything else. *(questioned thoroughly in order to reveal every bit of useful information they could remember)*

17. When I worked at Dell, we used to have to _____ every pencil we needed. *(ask for in writing)*

18. She reported that the incision was _____. *(causing no trouble or pain at the moment)*

19. The space traveler believed that what he had seen was an _____ vision. *(a look at the future that had been shown to him)*

20. Because of the car's _____, it kept going even when I took my foot off the accelerator. *(the rule of nature that keeps something moving once it gets started)*

Words to choose from: abyss, agonize, apocalyptic, bristled, chestnut, coincide, debriefed, differentiate, fundamentalist, holocaust, limbo, momentum, perspective, prerequisite, purge, pragmatist, quiescent, requisition, retinue, vicariously.

MINI-DICTIONARY

Some of these words have additional meanings in the same or another part of speech. In most cases we include just the most widely used meaning or meanings and just one part of speech. (Pronunciation is from *Webster's 8th Collegiate,* though we've simplified diacritical style.)

abate (uh-BATE): *v.* to put an end to; to reduce in intensity, amount, or value

aberration (ab-uh-RAY-shun): *n.* a deviation from the normal, the usual, or the natural way; unsoundness or disorder of the mind

abort (uh-BORT): *v.* to stop in the early stages; to bring forth prematurely; to end pregnancy before term

abstraction (ab-STRAK-shun): *n.* a summary or picture that makes no attempt at precise representation

abyss (uh-BIS): *n.* bottomless or immeasurably deep gulf or pit

accolade (AK-uh-lade): *n.* a mark or expression of praise

acrid (AK-rid): *adj.* unpleasantly strong in taste or odor; very bitter

acquisitor (uh-KWIZ-ut-er) *n.* someone who has acquired, especially library materials by purchase, exchange, or gift

acrimony (AK-ruh-moe-nee): *n.* harshly or bitingly sharp words or manner

acronym (AK-ruh-nim): *n.* a word formed from the first letter or letters of each word (or part) of a multi-word term

activist (AK-ti-vust): *adj.* acting strongly in support of or in opposition to one side of a controversial issue

acuity (a-KYU-it-ee): *n.* keenness of perception

ad lib (ad-LIB): *n.* something spoken, composed, or performed without preparation

adamant (AD-uh-munt): *adj.* unshakable or unmovable, especially in opposition

admonish (ad-MON-ish): *v.* to warn or disapprove gently, to tell of duties or obligations

admonition (ad-muh-NISH-un): *n.* gentle warning or disapproval

adulation (aj-uh-LAY-shun): *n.* excessive or slavish flattery or admiration

adversary (AD-ver-sair-ee): *n.* enemy or opponent

adversity (ad-VER-si-tee): *n.* condition of suffering, illness, or poverty; a calamitous or disastrous experience

affable (AF-uh-bull): *adj.* pleasant and at ease in talking to others; friendly

afflict (uh-FLIKT): *v.* to distress to the point of persistent suffering or anguish

aftermath (AF-ter-math): *n.* result; period after a usually ruinous event

agonize (AG-uh-nize): *v.* to suffer agony; to cause agony

alleged (uh-LEJD, uh-LEJ-uhd): *adj.* said to be true or to exist; questionably true or as specified

allegory (AL-uh-gore-ee): *n.* the telling of truths or generalizations about human experience through symbolic fictional characters and actions; a symbolic representation

alleviate (uh-LEE-vee-ate): *v.* to partially remove or correct; to make more bearable

altruistic (al-true-IS-tick): *adj.* unselfishly devoted to the welfare of others

amalgam (uh-MAL-gum): *n.* a mixture of different elements

ambivalence (am-BIV-uh-lunss): *n.* simultaneous attraction and revulsion; continual fluctuation; uncertainty as to which approach to follow

amorphous (uh-MORE-fuss): *adj.* having no definite shape, character or nature; lacking organization or unity

analogous (uh-NAL-uh-guss): *adj.* showing a resemblance in some ways even though being otherwise unlike

anathema (uh-NATH-uh-muh): *n.* a curse; someone cursed by church authorities; someone who is intensely disliked

anguish (ANG-gwish): *n.* extreme pain in body or mind

animosity (an-uh-MAHSS-utt-ee): *n.* ill will or resentment tending toward active hostility

annexation (an-ek-SAY-shun): *n.* the attachment of one thing to another

annihilate (uh-NY-uh-late): *v.* to destroy; to cease to exist; to cause to be of no effect

anodyne (AN-uh-dine): *n.* something that soothes or comforts; a drug that allays pain

anomaly (uh-NAHM-uh-lee): *n.* deviation from what's normal or common

anonymity (an-uh-NIM-uht-ee): *n.* the quality of having or giving no name

antagonize (an-TAG-uh-nize): *v.* to act in opposition to; to provoke hostility

ante (ANT-ee): *n.* an amount paid

apathy (AP-uh-thee): *n.* lack of feeling or emotion; lack of interest or concern

apocalypse (uh-POCK-uh-lips): *n.* time when God will destroy the rulers of evil and raise the righteous to heaven; something seen as a prophetic revelation

apotheosis (uh-pahth-ee-OH-suhs): *n.* (*pl.* apotheoses) elevation to divine status; a perfect example

appalling (uh-PAWL-ing): *adj.* causing horror, dismay, or disgust

appreciable (uh-PREE-shuh-buhl): *adj.* able to be measured

approbation (ap-ruh-BAY-shun): *n.* formal or official approval or praise

arbitrary (AHR-buh-trair-ee): *adj.* selected at random and without reason; behaving unjustly and oppressively; capricious or high-handed

arcane (ahr-KANE): *adj.* known only to one who has the key; secret, mysterious, supernatural

argot (AHR-gut, AHR-go): *n.* a more or less secret dialect

articulate (ahr-TICK-yuh-late): *v.* to utter distinctly and clearly; to unite by means of a joint; to form or fit into a systematic whole

aspect (ASS-pekt): *n.* appearance; particular way in which something may be looked at

aspirant (ASS-puh-runt, uh-SPY-runt): *n.* one who seeks a desired position or status

assess (uh-SESS): *v.* to determine the rate, amount, size, value, or importance of; to impose or subject to a tax; to evaluate property in order to tax it

assimilate (uh-SIMM-uh-late): *v.* to absorb into the system, especially as nourishment, or into the group or culture; to take into the mind and understand thoroughly; to make similar

assuage (uh-SWAYJ): *v.* to lessen pain or distress; to quiet; to put an end to by satisfying

attaché (at-uh-SHAY, AT-TA-shay): *n.* technical expert attached to a foreign wing of his country's diplomatic staff

attributable (uh-TRIB-yuht-uh-bull): *adj.* able to be regarded as belonging to a person or thing

audacious (aw-DAY-shuss): *adj.* recklessly bold or daring; contemptuous of law, religion, or decorum; marked by lively originality

augur (AW-guhr): *v.* to foretell the future, especially from omens; to give promise

augment (awg-MENT): *v.* to add to something that's already well or adequately developed

austere (aw-STEER): *adj.* appearing stern and forbidding; unadorned, simple; somber

authenticator (aw-THENNT-i-kay-tuhr): *n.* something that proves the truth or genuineness of something else

autonomous (aw-TAHN-uh-muss): *adj.* marked by or having the right of self-government; existing; capable of existing, or being carried on independently, without outside control

avatar (AV-uh-tahr): *n.* an incarnation in human form; an embodiment; one version or phase of a continuing entity

avidly (AV-id-lee): *adv.* with keen eagerness; with consuming greed

backlash (BACK-lash): *n.* sudden violent backward movement; strong negative reaction

banal (buh-NAL, BANE-uhl): *adj.* lacking originality; common, ordinary

bastion (BASS-chun): *n.* a projecting part of a fortification; a fortified area; a stronghold

belie (bih-LIE): *v.* to give a false impression; to contrast with; to contradict

bellicose (BELL-ih-kose): *adj.* favoring or inclined to start wars or quarrels

belligerent (buh-LIDJ-uh-runt): *adj.* waging war; hostile, warlike

beneficiary (ben-uh-FISH-ee-ary): *n.* one who benefits from something; person named to receive benefits, especially monetary

beset (bih-SET): *v.* to trouble, set upon, or hem in

bifurcate (BUY-fuhr-kate, buy-FUHR-kate): *v.* to divide into two branches or parts

bilateral (buy-LAT-uh-ruhl, buy-LATT-ruhl): *adj.* having two sides; affecting two sides or parties

bland *adj.* smooth and soothing; showing no personal concern or embarrassment; dull

blatant (BLATE-nt): *adj.* offensively noisy; offensively conspicuous

blitzkrieg (BLITS-kreeg): *n.* war conducted with great speed or force; sudden or violent overpowering bombardment

bogus (BOW-guss): *adj.* not genuine

boisterous (BOY-struhss): *adj.* rowdy, stormy, marked by exuberant high spirits

bolster (BOWL-ster): *v.* to support; to boost

boycott (BOY-cott): *n.* refusal by a group to have dealings with, usually to show disapproval or to force acceptance of certain conditions

bristle (BRISS-uhl): *v.* to take on an aggressive attitude or appearance

broach *v.* to open up or break into; to open a subject for discussion

bruit about (BREWT-uh-BOWT): *v.* to tell and retell a rumor or report

bumbling (BUM-buh-ling): *adj.* stumbling; speaking in a faltering or stuttering way

buoy (BOO-ee, BOY): *v.* to keep afloat; to support; to raise someone's spirits

burnish (BUHRN-ish): *v.* to rub with a smoothing tool; to make shiny, especially by rubbing

calamitous (kuh-LAMM-uht-uss): *adj.* causing or being accompanied by major misfortune, great loss, or lasting misery

candor (KAN-duhr, KAN-dore): *n.* honesty, sincerity; openness; freedom from prejudice or malice

cap: *v.* to provide with a cap; to outdo

cardinal (KARD-nuhl, KARD-uh-nuhl): *adj.* of basic importance

careen (ka-REEN): *v.* to sway from side to side

cataclysmic (kat-uh-KLIZ-mick): *adj.* disastrous, marked by overwhelming upheaval and demolition

catalytic (cat-uhl-IT-ick): *adj.* causing or involving an action or reaction between persons or forces, in which the causer is unchanged by the reaction

causal (CAW-zuhl): *adj.* arising from a cause, showing cause

centenary (sen-TEN-uh-ree, SENT-uhn-er-ee): *n.* hundredth anniversary

chagrined (shuh-GRINND): *v.* acutely disappointed or embarrassed

chestnut (CHES-nutt): *n.* an old joke or story; something that's been repeated so often it's stale

chicanery (shik-AYN-uh-ree): *n.* trickery; a trick

chronic (KRONN-ik): *adj.* marked by long duration, frequent occurrence; ever-present; done through habit

circumspection (suhr-kum-SPEK-shun): *n.* consideration of all possible consequences and circumstances; cautiousness

circumvent (suhr-kuhm-VENT): *v.* to detour around, to hem in, to stop or defeat with ingenuity or strategy

clout (KLOWT): *n.* a blow with the hand; influence

coherent (ko-HERE-ent): *adj.* holding together, being logically consistent, making sense

cohesive (ko-HE-sivv): *adj.* tightly sticking together

coincide (ko-uhn-SIDE): *v.* to occupy the same space or time; to be in agreement

collateral (kuh-LATT-uh-ruhl): *adj.* accompanying but subordinate; serving to support or reinforce; indirect

colloquial (kuh-LOH-kwee-uhl): *adj.* conversational; used in or characteristic of informal conversation

comply (kum-PLY): *v.* to conform or adapt one's actions

conciliatory (kuhn-SILL-yuh-tore-ee): *adj.* attempting to please to gain good will; being friendly or agreeable

condescending (kahn-di-SEN-ding): *adj.* assuming an air of superiority; descending to a less dignified level

confrontation (kahn-fruhn-TAY-shun): *n.* face-to-face meeting; clash of forces or ideas

congenital (kuhn-JEN-uh-tl): *adj.* existing at or from birth; being such by nature; developed in the uterus rather than by heredity

conjecture (kuhn-JECK-chuhr): *n.* conclusion made on slight grounds or by guesswork

consecrate (KAHN-suh-krate): *v.* to devote to a sacred purpose; to devote to a purpose with deep dedication; to make sacred or venerable

contentious (kuhn-TEN-chuss): *adj.* likely to cause argument; enjoying argument

context (KAHN-text): *n.* surrounding words that can throw light on a passage's meaning; surroundings

contingent (kuhn-TIN-juhnt): *adj.* likely to happen; happening by chance; dependent on something else

contingent: *n.* troop

contretemps (KAHN-truh-tahnh): *n. (sing. or pl.)* an embarrassing or inconvenient occurrence

contrition (kuhn-TRISH-uhn): *n.* the act of becoming sorry for sins or shortcomings

convoluted (KAHN-vuh-loot-uhd): *adj.* folded in curved or twisted windings; twisted, intricate, involved

co-opt (koh-OPPT): *v.* to take into a group; to take over

cordon off (KORD-n-awff): *v.* to form a restrictive line around something

cornerstone (KOR-nuhr-stone): *n.* the most basic element

cosmetic (kozz-MET-ick): *adj.* beautifying; correcting defects, especially superficial ones

coup (KOO): *n.* a brilliant, sudden, and usually very successful act

credible (KRED-uh-buhl): *adj.* offering reasonable grounds for being believed

crocodile (KROCK-uh-dile): *adj.* showing false sorrow (from *crocodile tears,* meaning false or affected tears)

crudity (KROOD-uh-tee): *n.* vulgarity; state of being rude or uncultured

cuckold (KUHK-uhld): *n.* a man whose wife is unfaithful

cull (KULL): *v.* to select from a group

culpable (KUHL-puh-buhl): *adj.* worthy of blame for acting wrong or harmfully

curb (kerb): *v.* to furnish with a curb; to check or control

curtail (ker-TAIL): *v.* to make less, to cut short

debrief (dih-BREEF, dee-BREEF): *v.* to question in order to obtain useful information; to instruct not to reveal any classified information after release from a sensitive position

default (dih-FAWLT): *v.* to fail to perform, pay, or make good; to forfeit a contest by such failure

deficit (DEFF-uh-suht): *n.* a deficiency or loss in amount or quality; a business loss; a disadvantage

defile (dih-FILE, dee-FILE): *v.* to corrupt; to make physically or ceremonially unclean or impure

deftly: *adv.* skillfully

degenerate (dih-JENN-uh-ruht): *adj.* having declined from an ancestral or former state; having sunk to a lower, usually corrupt and vicious condition; having gotten worse or gone wrong

demean (dih-MEEN): *v.* to lower in status; belittle

demeanor (dih-MEEN-orr): *n.* outward manner, behavior toward others

denunciation (dih-NUN-see-AY-shun): *n.* act of publicly condemning or accusing

deployment (dih-PLOY-muhnt): *n.* placement in battle formation; act of being used, arranged, or spread out, especially strategically

derelict (DEHR-uh-likt): *adj.* abandoned, especially by the owner or occupant; lacking a sense of duty

derelict: *n.* castoff, outcast, or bum

derisive (dih-RY-sihv): *adj.* expressing or causing ridicule or scorn

desiccate (DESS-ih-kate): *v.* to dry up, to preserve by drying, to become dried up; to become drained of emotional or intellectual vitality

desultory (DESS-uhl-tore-ee, DEZ-uhl-tore-ee): *adj.* marked by lack of definite plan, regularity, or purpose; not connected with the main subject

détente (day-TAHNHT): *n.* relaxation of strained relations or tensions

deter (dih-TUHR): *v.* to turn aside, discourage, or prevent from acting

detrimental (deh-truh-MENT-uhl): *adj.* obviously harmful

detritus (dih-TREE-tuss): *n., sing. or pl.* a product (especially loose material) resulting from disintegration or wearing away

differentiate (diff-uh-REN-chee-ate): *v.* to develop or show a difference; to recognize a difference

dilatory (DILL-uh-toe-ree): *adj.* tending or intended to cause delay; being delayed or put off

diligent (DILL-uh-juhnt): *adj.* showing steady, earnest, energetic effort

dint: *n.* force (*by dint of:* because of)

disavow (dis-uh-VOW): *v.* to refuse to acknowledge; to deny responsibility for

disciple (diss-I-puhl): *n.* a follower, a person who helps spread someone else's ideas

disclaimer (diss-KLAME-uhr): *n.* a denial of legal claim; a formal refusal, denial, or surrendering of rights

disconcerting (diss-kuhn-SER-ting): *adj.* disturbing the composure or throwing into confusion; embarrassing

disparity (diss-PAR-uh-tee): *n.* difference

dissident (DISS-uhd-uhnt): *n.* one who disagrees with an opinion or a group

dissuade (diss-WADE): *v.* to advise someone against something; to turn away by persuasion

divergent (duh-VUHRJ-uhnt): *adj.* differing from each other or from a standard

diverting (duh-VUHRT-ing): *adj.* pleasing, especially by distracting attention from what burdens or distresses

divisive (duh-VI-sivv, duh-VISS-iv): *adj.* creating disunity or disagreement

doddering (DODD-uh-ring): *adj.* old and feeble, senile, foolish

domineering (dom-uh-NEAR-ing): *adj.* assuming strong and arbitrary control over another; tyrannizing

drab: *adj.* dull brown in color; monotonously dull

dubious (DYU-bee-us): *adj.* giving rise to doubt, undecided in opinion; doubtful or undecided in outcome, of questionable value or origin

duplicitous (dyu-PLISS-uht-uss): *adj.* using deceptive words or actions to mask one's true intentions

eclipse (ih-KLIPS): *v.* reduce in importance or reputation, obscure or darken;

ecological (ee-kuh-LODJ-ih-kuhl): *adj.* having to do with the relationship between organisms and their environment

educe (ih-DYUSE): *v.* to bring out; to deduce

efficacy (EF-ih-kuh-see): *n.* effectiveness

effectively (ih-FEK-tihv-lee): *adj.* actually, substantially; to all intents and purposes

elicit (ih-LISS-uht): *v.* to draw forth or bring out; to derive logically

elusive (ee-LU-sihv): *adj.* evading grasp or pursuit; hard to understand, define, isolate or identify

embargo (em-BAR-goh): *n.* a prohibition; a legal or governmental prohibition on commerce or freight transportation

empirical (ihm-PEER-ih-kuhl): *adj.* relying on or based on experience or observation; capable of being proved by experience or observation

engineer (en-juh-NEAR): *v.* to guide the course of; to plan out, usually with some skill

enigma (ih-NIG-muh): *n.* something hard to explain or understand; a mysterious or hard-to-understand person

enterprise (EN-ter-prize): *n.* a hard, complicated, or risky project; a systematic activity, especially a business activity; willingness to engage in daring action

entitlement (ihn-TITE-uhl-ment): *n.* the papers or other grounds that support a claim

entity (ENHT-uh-tee): *n.* something that exists independently or separately; the existence of a thing as contrasted with its attributes

entrepreneur (AHN-truh-pruh-NYURE): *n.* one who organizes, manages, and assumes the risks of a business or enterprise

envoy (ENN-voy, AHN-voy): *n.* a person delegated to represent one country in dealings with another; a messenger or representative

epicenter (EP-ee-sent-uhr): *n.* center; part of the earth's surface directly above an earthquake

epiphany (ih-PIFF-uh-nee): *n.* an appearance, especially of a divine being; a sudden understanding of the essential meaning or nature of something; an intuitive grasp of reality through something simple and striking, usually an event

epochal (EP-uh-kuhl): *adj.* seasonal; uniquely or highly significant; opening a new era

equilibrium (ee-kwi-LIB-ree-um): *n.* state of balance between different elements; intellectual or emotional balance

erratic (ihr-AT-ick): *adj.* having no fixed course; inconsistent, irregular, or without uniformity; deviating from what's ordinary or standard

escalate (ES-kuh-late): *v.* to increase in amount or intensity

escapism (iss-KA-pizm): *n.* habitual diversion of the mind to entertainment or imaginative activity as an escape from reality or routine

espouse (iss-POWZ, iss-POWSS): *v.* to marry; to take up and support a cause

estuary (ESSH-chu-ware-ee): *n.* a water passage where the tide meets a river current, especially where the sea meets the river

euphemism (YU-fuh-mizz-uhm): *n.* the substitution of an agreeable or inoffensive expression for an unpleasant or offensive one; the expression so substituted

euphoria (yu-FOR-ee-uh): *n.* feeling of well-being or elation

evasive (ih-VAY-sivv): *n.* tending or intended to avoid giving a direct answer

eventuality (ih-venn-chuh-WAL-uht-ee): *n.* possible outcome

evoke (ih-VOKE): *v.* to call forth, bring to mind; to cite, especially with approval or for support

exact (ihg-ZAKT): *v.* to demand and obtain; to call for as necessary, appropriate, and desirable

ex cathedra (ek-skuh-THAY-druh): *adv., adj.* (literally, *from the chair*) proceeding from or in the exercise of one's job or office; with authority

excessive (ik-SESS-ihv): *adj.* exceeding the usual, proper, or normal

exemplify (ig-ZEMM-pluh-fy): *v.* to illustrate by example; to serve as an example; to be typical of

exonerate (ig-ZONN-uh-rate): *v.* to relieve from responsibility; to clear from blame

exorbitant (ig-ZOR-buht-uhnt): *adj.* exceeding customary or appropriate limits

expatriate (ek-SPAY-tree-ate): *v.* to leave or renounce one's country; to drive into exile, to banish

explicit (ik-SPLISS-it): *adj.* fully developed; free from vagueness; externally visible

exploit (ik-SPLOYT, EK-sployt): *v.* to take advantage of; to turn to economic advantage; to use unjustly or meanly for one's own advantage

expropriate (ek-SPROH-pree-ate): *v.* to deprive of possession or ownership; to transfer another's property to one's own possession

extrapolate (ik-STRAP-uh-late): *v.* to protect from observed values; to predict using past experience or known data

extraterrestrial (ek-struh-tuh-RESS-tree-uhl): *adj.* originating or existing outside the earth and its atmosphere

exultant (ig-ZULT-uhnt): *adj.* filled with or showing great joy or triumph

facade (fuh-SAHD): *n.* the front of a building, or any other of its faces given special architectural treatment; a superficial, artificial, or false appearance or effect

faction (FAK-shun): *n.* a party or group within a larger group, often self-seeking or warring with the rest of the group

falter (FALL-tuhr): *v.* to move or speak waveringly, hesitatingly, or weakly; to lose drive or effectiveness

fandango (fan-DANg-goh): *n.* a lively Spanish dance; foolish nonsense

farcical (FAR-si-kuhl): *adj.* ridiculous; absurd; mocking; laughably inept

fare (FAYR): *v.* to travel; to get along; to eat

fathom (FATH-uhm): *v.* to take soundings; to penetrate and come to understand

fecklessness (FECK-luhs-nuhs): *n.* weakness; lack of effectiveness; lack of worth or responsibility

feign (FANE): *v.* to give a false impression; to pretend

ferret (FERR-uht): *v.* (usually used with *out*) to find and bring to light by searching

fervent (FUHR-vent): *adj.* very hot; marked by great warmth of feeling

fete (FATE, FETT): *n.* festival; large elaborate party

fiasco (fee-ASS-koh): *n.* a complete failure

fiscal (FISS-kuhl): *adj.* relating to financial matters, especially taxation

flamboyant (flam-BOY-uhnt): *adj.* ornate; given to showy display

fledgling (FLEDJ-ling): *adj.* immature, inexperienced

fluctuation (fluck-chuh-WAY-shun): *n.* an uncertain shifting back and forth

fluke: *n.* a stroke of luck

fob off: *v.* to put off with a trick or excuse; to pass off as genuine; to put aside

foil: *n.* a person or thing that makes another seem better by contrast

foment (fo-MENNT): *v.* to treat with moist heat; to heat up, especially in helping something grow

foray (FOR-ay, FOH-ray): *n.* a sudden or irregular raid; a brief trip outside one's usual territory

formidable (FOR-muhd-uh-buhl, for-MIDD-uh-buhl): *adj.* causing fear or dread; having qualities that discourage approach; tending to inspire awe

formulation (for-myuh-LAY-shun): *n.* act or product of putting into a systematized statement or formula

foster (FOSS-tuhr): *v.* to give parental care to; to promote the growth or development of

founder: *v.* to become disabled; to give way; to sink below the water's surface; to come to grief

fruitless: *adj.* unsuccessful

fundamentalist (fun-duh-MENT-uh-list): *n.* one who believes in strictly and literally following a set of basic principles; a member of a 20th century Protestant group that emphasizes a literal interpretation of the Bible

furor: (FYU-roar): *n.* an angry rage; a fashionable craze; furious or hectic activity; a public uproar

gaffe (GAFF): *n.* a social error

galvanized (GAL-vuh-nized): *adj.* stimulated by or as if by an electric shock; coated with zinc

gambit (GAM-bit): *n.* a calculated move; a remark intended to start a conversation or make a point

garb: *n.* style of dress; outward appearance

gargantuan (gar-GANCH-uh-wuhn): *adj.* of tremendous size or volume

garrulousness (GAR-uh-luhs-nuss, GAR-yuh-luhs-nuss): *n.* pointless or annoying talkativeness

gibe (JIBE): *n.* taunting words; a teasing remark

goad (GODE): *n.* a pointed rod used to urge on an animal; something that pricks; something that urges or stimulates into action

grandiose (GRAN-di-ohse, gran-di-OHSE): *adj.* impressively large or great; characterized by affectation. of grandeur or splendor; absurdly exaggerated

grasp: *n.* act of seizing and holding; understanding

gratuitous (gruh-TYU-uht-uss): *adj.* given unearned or without payment; costing nothing; not called for by the circumstances

grievance (GREE-vuhnts): *n.* a distressing situation felt as reason for complaint or resistance; a complaint

gross (GROSE): *adj.* glaringly noticeable, usually because of inexcusable badness or bad taste; big, very fat; unrefined, crudely vulgar

ground swell: *n.* a broad deep ocean wave caused by a gale or earthquake; a rapid spontaneous growth

grouse (GROWSS): *v.* complain, grumble

gyrate (JY-rate): *v.* to revolve around an axis; to turn with (or as if with) a circular or spiral motion

hamper: *v.* to interfere with; to keep from moving by way of obstacles or bonds

hanker (HANG-ker): *v.* to desire strongly or persistently

harangue (huh-RANG): *v.* to speak or write, especially in a noisy or pretentious manner

harass (huh-RASS, HAR-uhs): *v.* to worry and impede by repeated raids; to keep annoying; to exhaust

hawkish: *adj.* supporting immediate strong action, especially war or warlike policy

heartland: *n.* a central and vital area

hinterland (HINT-uhr-land): *n.* an inland region; a region remote from cities, or from major cultural centers

hodgepodge (HODGE-podge): *n.* a mixture of unrelated things

hokum (HO-kumm): *n.* a device used to create a desired audience response; pretentious nonsense

holocaust (HOLL-uh-kawst, HO-luh-kawst): *n.* a thorough destruction, especially by fire

hustings (HUSS-tings): *n.* in some places in England and Virginia, a local court; an election platform; the proceedings or place of an election campaign

hustle (HUSS–uhl): *v.* to convey or urge forward forcibly or hurriedly; to make great effort to secure money or business; to sell or get something by energetic activity, especially by fraud or deception

hypothetical (hy-puh-THET-i-kull): *adj.* depending on supposition; not verifiable

immediacy (im-EED-ee-uh-see): *n.* need to do or be done at once; act of being current, in the here and now

imminent (IMM-uh-nent): *adj.* ready to take place (especially used of a threatening possible occurrence)

impair (im-PAIR): *v.* to make physically worse

impeccable (im-PECK-uh-buhl) *adj.* not capable of sinning; free from fault or blame

imperative (im-PERR-uht-iv): *n.* an act or duty that must be done; a command, order, rule or guide

implacably (im-PLAK-uh-blee): *adv.* unable to be made calmer, less angry, or changed in some other way

implicit (im-PLISS-uht): *adj.* implied; within something's nature though not revealed, expressed, or developed; unquestioning, unhesitating

imponderable (im-PONN-duh-ruh-buhl): *adj.* unable to be weighed or evaluated with exactness

impose (im-POZE): *v.* to establish by force; to establish as compulsory; to force into the company or attention of someone; to take advantage

impotent (IM-pote-uhnt): *adj.* lacking power, strength or vigor; sterile

inadvertence (in-uhd-VERT-uhnss): *n.* inattention; accidental oversight; the result of inattention

incapacitate (in-kuh-PASS-uh-tate): *v.* to disable; to make legally incapable or ineligible

incarnation (in-kar-NAY-shun): *n.* embodiment of a spirit in earthly form; time passed in a particular body or state; having a quality to a marked degree

incendiary (in-SEN-dee-air-ee): *adj.* relating to deliberate burning of property; tending to excite or inflame

incinerate (in-SIN-uh-rate): *v.* to cause to burn to cinders

incoherent (in-co-HERE-uhnt): *adj.* lacking orderly arrangement; not sticking together in an orderly way

incorrigible (in-KAWR-uh-juh-buhl): *adj.* not correctible; not reformable; uncontrollable

incur (in-KUHRR): *v.* to bring down upon oneself; to become liable or subject to

indigent (IN-dih-juhnt): *adj.* suffering poverty so severe, all the comforts of life are lacking

indiscreet (in-dis-KRETE): *adj.* lacking good judgment in conduct or speech

indissoluble (in-dis-OLL-yuh-buhl): *adj.* incapable of being dissolved or decomposed; incapable of being broken or undone, permanent

individualist (in-duh-VIDJ-wuh-list): *n.* a person whose thoughts or actions are independent; a person who believes that the interests of individual people are of greatest importance

ineffectual (in-uh-FECK-chuh-wuhl): *adj.* ineffective; not producing the intended effect

ineptitude (in-EP-tuh-tyude): *n.* lack of competence

inequity (in-EK-wuh-tee): *n.* injustice, unfairness

inevitable (in-EV-uh-tuh-buhl): *adj.* unable to be avoided

infamy (IN-fuh-mee): *n.* a criminal or evil act that's publicly known; a bad reputation produced by doing something shocking, brutal, or criminal

influx (IN-flucks): *n.* a flowing in

infused (in-FYUZED): *adj.* completely filled with or affected by something, usually for the better

ingenuity (in-juh-NYU-uh-tee): *n.* cleverness in devising or designing something; a clever device or design

ingratiating (in-GRAY-shee-ate-ing): *adj.* capable of winning favor; intended to win favor

initiative (in-ISH-uh-tivv): *n.* an introductory step; energy or aptitude shown by beginning an action; the right to begin legislative action, or the procedure that begins legislative action

innocuous (in-OCK-yew-uss): *adj.* harmless; unlikely to give offense or to arouse strong feelings, especially of hostility

innuendo (in-yew-WEN-doh): *n.* a hint or insinuation, especially against character or reputation

insatiable (in-SAY-shuh-buhl): *adj.* incapable of being satisfied

insouciance (in-SOO-see-uhnss): *n.* lighthearted unconcern; indifference

inspire: *v.* to affect, to motivate; to bring about, draw forth, or incite

instigate (IN-stuh-gate): *v.* to goad or urge forward

institute (IN-stuh-tyute): *v.* to establish, to set going

insurgency (in-SUHR-juhn-see): *n.* a condition of revolt against a government that's less than an organized revolution, and that isn't recognized as a war

integral (INT-ih-gruhl, in-TEG-ruhl): *adj.* formed as a unit with another part; being essential to completeness; lacking nothing essential

interim (INT-uh-ruhm): *adj.* intervening, temporary

interminably (in-TERM-uh-nuh-blee): *adv.* seemingly without end

internecine (int-er-NEES-een): *adj.* involving conflict within a group; marked by slaughter, especially when it's mutually destructive

interrogate (in-TERR-uh-gate): *v.* to question formally and systematically

intervene (int-uhr-veen): *v.* to come between; to interfere in another nation's internal affairs

intimidate (in-TIM-uh-date): *v.* to frighten; to compel with or as if with threats

intransigence (in-TRANTS-uh-JENTSS): *n.* refusal to compromise or to abandon an extreme position or attitude

intrusive (in-TRUE-sivv): *adj.* going or coming where one isn't wanted or invited; projecting forward

inured (in-YURED): *adj.* accustomed to accept something undesirable

invocation (in-vuh-KA-shun): *n.* the act of asking for help or support; a calling upon someone for authority or justification; a legal or moral enforcement

irrelevant (ir-RELL-uh-vuhnt): *adj.* beside the point

irreverent (ir-REV-uh-ruhnt, ir-REV-runt): *adj.* lacking proper respect in speech or action; joking or light in manner or quality

jape: *n.* something designed to amuse, especially something mocking

jest: *v.* to taunt; to speak or act without seriousness; to make a witty remark

jockey: *v.* to deal shrewdly or fraudulently with; to change position in a series of movements; to maneuver for advantage, especially by clever or devious means; to drive, operate

jubilant (JU-buh-luhnt): *adj.* filled with or showing great joy

junta (HUN-tuh, JUHN-tuh): *n.* a political or governmental committee, especially a group controlling a government after a revolutionary seizure of power

jurisdiction (juhr-uhs-DICK-shun): *n.* the power or right to interpret and apply the law; the authority of a power to govern; the limits within which authority may be exercised

kamikaze (kahm-ih-KAHZ-ee): *adj.* relating to a Japanese World War II air unit assigned to make suicidal crashes on targets; suicidal

klaxon (KLACK-suhn): *n.* an electrically operated horn or warning signal

laconic (luh-KAHN-ick): *adj.* using minimum words; concise to the point of seeming rude or mysterious

lambaste (also **lambast**) (LAM-baste, lam-BASTE): *v.* to asault violently; to attack verbally

lamentation (lamm-uhn-TAY-shun): *n.* a cry of grief

languor (LANg-goor): *n.* weakness or weariness of mind or body; listlessness, slowness, inertia

latent (LAYT-nt): *adj.* present invisibly or inactively but able to become visible or active

laud (LAWD): *v.* to praise

lavishly (LAV-ish-lee): *adj.* as if poured heavily; abundantly

lax: *adj.* not firm or rigid

laze: *v.* to pass the time idly or in relaxation

legacy (LEG-uh-see): *n.* a willed gift, especially of money or other personal property; something received from an ancestor, a predecessor, or the past

legitimacy (li-JIT-uh-muh-see): *n.* the quality of being lawful, lawfully gotten, or conforming to recognized principles or accepted rules and standards

levy (LEVV-ee): *n.* the collection of money; the amount raised by collection

lieu (LEW): *n.* place; *in lieu of:* instead of

limbo (LIMM-bow): *n.* place for souls barred from Heaven because unbaptized; place or state of confinement; an intermediate or transitional place or state

liquidation (lick-wuh-DAY-shun): *n.* a getting rid of, killing; a settlement of a debt; a conversion of assets into cash

litigation (lit-uh-GAY-shun): *n.* a legal dispute

litigious (luh-TIDGE-uss): *adj.* prone to start lawsuits; of, relating to, or marked by legal dispute

lodge: *v.* to settle in or occupy a place; to come to rest; to deposit for safeguard; to put before a proper authority

logjam: *n.* a jam-up of logs in a water course; a deadlock or impasse

ludicrous (LEWD-uh-kruhs): *adj.* amusing because of obvious absurdity or exaggeration; meriting scorn as being absurdly inept, false or foolish

lumps: *n.* beatings; deserved penalty

lustrous (LUHS-truss): *adj.* reflecting light evenly; radiant

macabre (muh-KAHB-re, muh-KAHB-er): *adj.* having to do with death, especially death represented as a person; dwelling on the gruesome; tending to cause horror in a beholder

magnific (mag-NIFF-ick): *adj.* magnificent; imposing in size or dignity; exalted; pompous

malice (MAL-uhs): *n.* desire to see another suffer; intent to act unlawfully or cause harm without legal justification or excuse

malign (muh-LINE): *adj.* evil in nature, influence, or effect; harmful; intensely and often viciously ill-willed

malign: *v.* to tell misleading false reports about; to speak badly of

mammoth (MAM-uth): *adj.* of great size

manipulate (muh-NIP-yuh-late): *v.* to handle or manage skillfully; to control or change by unfair or tricky means, especially to serve one's own purpose

marginal (MAHRJ-nuhl, MAHRJ-uh-nuhl): *adj.* located at the border; near the lower limit of acceptability or function

martial (MAR-shuhl): *adj.* relating to war, a warrior, the army, or military life; warlike

matinal (MAT-n-uhl): *adj.* early

mawkish: *adj.* having a dull, often unpleasant taste; being sickly or childishly sentimental

meander (me-AN-der): *v.* to follow a winding course; to wander casually

mediocre (meed-ee-OH-ker): *adj.* ordinary; inferior in quality

memorabilia (mem-uh-ruh-BILL-ee-uh): *n.* things worth remembering; records of such things

menial (ME-nee-yuhl): *adj.* relating to servants; lowly, humble; lacking interest or dignity

mentor (MEN-tore, MEN-ter): *n.* a trusted counselor, tutor, coach, or guide

mercurial (muhr-KYUR-ee-uhl): *adj.* having rapid and unpredictable mood changes

metaphor (MET-uh-fore, MET-uh-fer): *n.* a substitution of one word or phrase for another in order to express a similarity between the two ideas dealt with in the substitution

methodology (meth-uh-DOLL-uh-gee): *n.* a particular procedure or set of procedures; the analysis of the principles or procedures of inquiry in a particular field

meticulous (muh-TICK-yuh-luss): *adj.* extremely or excessively careful in handling details

millennium (muh-LENN-ee-uhm): *n*. a thousand years; a thousandth anniversary; the thousand years predicted in the Bible during which Christ will reign on Earth; a period of great happiness or human perfection

mimic (MIM-ick): *v*. to imitate; to ridicule by imitation

minuscule (also **miniscule**) (MIN-uhs-kyule): *adj*. very small

miscalculation *n*. mistake in figuring

moderate (MAHD-uh-rate): *v*. to lessen in intensity or extremeness; to act as chairman of

mogul (MOW-gull): *n*. a great person; a bump in a ski run

momentum (mow-MENT-uhm, muh-MENT-uhm): *n*. the property of a moving body or action that keeps it moving unless acted on by an outside force

monologist (muh-NAHL-uh-just, MAHN-uh-log-ist) (also **monologuist**) (MAHN-uhlog-ist): *n*. one who gives one or more solo dramatic speeches; one who monopolizes conversation with long speeches

moratorium (more-uh-TORE-ee-um): *n*. a waiting period set by an authority, especially a delay in debt payment; a suspension of activity

mordant (MORD-nt, more-DENT): *adj*. biting and caustic, incisive; burning, pungent

moribund (MORE-uh-bund): *adj*. being in a state of dying

mortification (mort-uh-fuh-KAY-shun): *n*. denial of the body's needs by abstinence or discomfort; humiliation and shame caused by something that hurts the pride or self-respect; the cause of such shame

mount: *v*. to increase in amount; to lift up, get up, go up; to launch and carry out

muck: *n*. moist manure; slimy dirt, mud; slanderous or unflattering remarks or writing

mufti (MUFF-tee): *n*. civilian clothes

municipality (myu-niss-uh-PAL-uh-tee): *n*. a political unit that's incorporated and usually governs itself

muted (MYEWT-uhd): *adj*. toned down, quieted, silent

myriad (MERE-ee-uhd): *adj*. a great many; being uncountable

negotiate (ni-GO–shee-ate): *v*. to confer in order to settle a matter, especially by compromise; to deal with; to successfully travel over, complete, or accomplish; to convert into cash

nettle: *v*. to sting; to arouse to sharp fleeting annoyance or anger

noncommittal (nahn-kuh-MIT-l): *adj*. giving no clear indication of attitude or feeling; having no clear character

nostrum (NAHS-trumm): *n*. questionable or ineffective remedy or scheme; secretly formulated medicine recommended by its preparer but usually without scientific proof of its effectiveness

nurture (NER-cher): *v*. to supply with nourishment; to further the development of; to educate

obliging (uh-BLY-jing): *adj*. willing to do favors; accommodating

obliquely (oh-BLEEK-lee): *adv*. at an angle; not straightforwardly; indirectly; underhandedly

obliterate (uh-BLIT-uh-rate): *v*. to obscure or wear away; to remove all trace; to cancel; to remove from memory; to make unrecognizable

obsolete (ahb-suh-LETE, AHB-suh-lete): *n*. no longer in use; outmoded

obstructionist (uhb-STRUCK-shun-ist): *n.* one who deliberately interferes with progress or business, especially that of a legislative body

ocher (also **ochre**) (OH-ker): *n.* an earthy red-yellow pigment made from iron ore; a muddy red-yellow color

offensive (uh-FENT-sivv): *n.* an attack

officious (uh-FISH-uhs): *adj.* meddlesome, offering one's services where neither wanted nor needed

oligarch (AHL-uh-gark, OH-luh-gark): *n.* a member or supporter of government by a small group, especially one that controls for selfish purposes

ominous (AHM-uh-nuss): *adj.* warning or foretelling, especially of something bad to come

orgy (OR-jee): *n.* drunken partying; a sexually abandoned party; an action or event that shows abandon or lack of control

ostensibly (ah-STENT-suh-blee): *adv.* apparently; in appearance, though not necessarily in fact

oust: *v.* to remove from position, authority, or property rights, especially by force or legal action; to take the place of

outmoded: *adj.* no longer stylish, usable, or acceptable

overarching: *adj.* forming an overhead arch; all-embracing; dominating

overextension (oh-vuh-rick-STEN-shun): *n.* commitment, especially financially, beyond a safe or reasonable point

overt (oh-VERT, OH-vert): *adj.* open to view

pacifist (PASS-uh-fuhst): *n.* one who is opposed to war or violence as a means of settling disputes, or who refuses to bear arms; one who refuses to resist actively

palaver (puh-LAV-uhr, puh-LAHV-uhr): *n.* a long talk, usually between persons of different cultures; idle or misleading talk

panacea (pan-uh-SEE-uh): *n.* a cure-all

Panglossian (pan-GLOSS-ee-uhn): *adj.* believing that everything happens for the best and this is the best of all possible worlds

paradigm (PAR-uh-dime, PAR-uh-dimm): *n.* an especially clear or typical example

paradox (PAR-uh-dox): *n.* a statement that seems contradictory yet may be true; a self-contradictory statement that seems true at first; something or someone with seemingly contradictory qualities or phases

parity (PAR-uh-tee): *n.* being equal or having the same value, especially in buying power

parochial (puh-RO-kee-uhl): *adj.* relating to a church parish; confined or restricted to a parish; limited in range or scope

parody (PAR-uh-dee): *n.* a close imitation for comic or ridiculing effect; a poor or silly imitation

pedestrian (puh-DESS-tree-uhn): *adj.* going on foot; related to walking; commonplace, unimaginative

peevish: *adj.* ill-tempered, obstinate

penchant (PEN-chuhnt): *n.* a strong liking

penury (PEN-yuh-ree): *n.* oppressive lack of resources, especially extreme poverty; extreme and often stingy care in spending money

perceive (per-SEEVE): *v.* to become aware of or understand, especially through the senses

perfunctory (per-FUNCK-tuh-ree): *adj.* performed routinely, mechanically, or unwillingly; lacking in interest or enthusiasm

permeate (PER-mee-ate): *v.* to spread throughout

perspective (per-SPECK-tivv): *n.* the way something is seen, especially with respect to relative distance and position; the ability to view things in true relation or relative importance

pervade (per-VADE): *v.* to spread through every part

perverse (per-VERSE): *n.* turned away from what is good, correct, or proper; obstinate, expecially in opposing what is right or accepted; cranky; contrary to evidence

phalanx (FAY-lanks): *n.* body of close-standing troops; a massed arrangement of persons, animals, or things; an organized group of persons

pilfer (PILL-fer): *v.* to steal, usually stealthily and over and over, in small amounts

plausible (PLAW-zuh-buhl): *adj.* seemingly worthy of belief; seeming fair or reasonable

plethora (PLETH-uh-ruh): *n.* an excess

ploy: *n.* a tactic, especially one designed to embarrass or frustrate an opponent; something devised or contrived

podium (PODE-ee-um): *n.* a platform for an orchestra conductor; a small table on which to rest speaker's notes; a place of formality

poignant (POY-nyuhnt): *adj.* deeply or painfully affecting; pleasurably stimulating; cutting; to the point

polarization (po-luh-ruh-ZA-shun): *n.* division into two opposites, especially opposite factions or groups

polymathic (poll-ih-MATH-ic): *adj.* having or showing encyclopedic knowledge; very learned

ponder (PAHN-der): *v.* to think about, especially quietly, soberly, and deeply; to weigh in the mind

populist (POP-yuh-luhst): *n.* a believer in the rights, wisdom, or virtues of the common people

portage (POR-ihj): *v.* to move gear, especially overland from one body of water to another

portend (por-TEND): *v.* to signify; to give an omen of

posh: *adj.* elegant; fashionable

postulate (PAHS-chuh-late): *v.* to demand; to claim, especially to claim as true, existent, or necessary

potent (POTE-nt): *adj.* powerful; effective

pragmatist (PRAG-muht-ist): *n.* one who believes in taking a practical approach to things

prattle: *n.* chatter, empty talk

precipice (PRESS-uh-puhs): *n.* a very steep or overhanging place; the brink of disaster

precipitate (prih-SIP-uh-tate): *v.* to move or make happen abruptly; to come suddenly into some condition

preclude (pri-KLUDE): *v.* to prevent; to do something that makes another thing impossible

predecessor (PRED-uh-sess-uhr): *n.* one who has previously occupied a place that someone else now has

preemptive (pree-EMP-tivv): *adj.* taking the place of; taking for oneself; taking before others can do so; having the power to take for oneself or before others

preoccupied (pree-AHK-yuh-pide): *adj.* lost in thought

prerequisite (pree-RECK-wuh-zuht): *adj.* needed in order to carry out a function

presage (PRESS-idge, pri-SAGE): *v.* to warn or predict; to have a premonition of

primer (PRIMM-uhr): *n.* a small book for teaching children to read; a small introductory book on a subject

probe: *n.* a tool used in surgery to examine a cavity; a device used to explore or send information from outer space; a penetrating or critical investigation; a tentative exploration

problematic (prahb-luh-MAT-ick): *n.* puzzling, bewildering; unsettled; possible; open to question or debate

profess (pruh-FESS, proh-FESS): *v.* to declare or admit freely; to pretend; to claim to know

professed: *adj.* freely stated; pretended; claiming to be qualified

profound (pruh-FOUND): *adj.* coming from, reaching to, or being down deep; showing deep feeling; full of insight; hard to understand; complete

prohibitively (pro-HIB-uht-iv-lee): *adv.* tending to prevent or restrain; tending to prevent the use or acquisition of something

proliferate (pro-LIFF-uh-rate): *v.* to grow or cause to grow by rapid production of new parts; to multiply

prominent (PRAHM-uh-nent): *adj.* standing out beyond a surface; easily noticed; widely known

propensity (pruh-PEN-suht-ee): *adj.* a strong natural inclination

propound (pruh-POUND): *v.* to offer for discussion or consideration

proscribe (pro-SCRIBE): *v.* to publish the name of a person condemned to death with all property forfeited to the state; to condemn or forbid as harmful; to ostracize

protégé (PROTE-uh-zhay): *n.* one under the care and protection of an influential person, usually to further a career

province (PRAHV-uhnts): *n.* a division of a country; a proper or appropriate function; a sphere of knowledge, influence, or activity

provocative (pruh-VAHK-uht-ivv): *n.* tending to arouse, excite, or stimulate; tending to stimulate thought

prudent (PRUDE-nt): *adj.* marked by wisdom or sound judgment; discreet; shrewd in managing practical affairs

prune: *v.* to cut off parts for better growth; to cut away what isn't wanted

pseudo (SUDE-oh): *adj.* being false or make-believe

pseudonym (SUDE-n-im): *n.* false name, especially one used by a writer

puerile (PYUR-uhl, PYUR-ile): *adj.* young; childish, silly

puffery (PUFF-uh-ree): *n.* flattering, often exaggerated publicity

pullulate (PUHL-yuh-late): *v.* to sprout; to breed or produce freely; to swarm

punitive (PYU-nuht-ivv): *adj.* inflicting or aimed at punishment

purge (PERJ): *v.* to free, especially from guilt; to get rid of, especially because deemed undesirable, treacherous, or unloyal

purported (per-PORT-ed): *adj.* believed, rumored

putative (PYUT-uht-ivv): *adj.* commonly accepted or supposed; assumed to exist or to have existed

quantum (KWAHNT-uhm): (*pl.* quanta): *n.* particle of energy; amount, part

quantum jump, quantum leap: *n.* abrupt change or sudden increase

quest (KWEST): *n.* pursuit, search; investigation

quiescent (KWY-es-nt): *adj.* inactive; causing no trouble or symptoms

raffish: *adj.* marked by or suggesting flashy vulgarity or careless unconventionality

ramification (ram-uh-fuh-KA-shun): *n.* outgrowth or consequence

rapprochement (ra-prosh-MAHNH): *n.* an establishment of cordial relations

ratify (RAT-uh-fy): *v.* to formally approve

rationale (rash-uh-NAL): *n.* an explanation for a belief, practice, opinion, or happening; an underlying reason

raucous (RAW-kuss): *adj.* disagreeably harsh; noisily disorderly

recant (re-KANT): *v.* to openly confess an error; to publicly withdraw a statement or belief

reconstitute (re-KON-stuh-tyute): *v.* to restore to a former condition

redress (ri-DRESS, REE-dress): *v.* to set right; to make up for; to remove the cause of; to avenge

refute (ri-FYUTE): *v.* to disprove with argument or evidence; to deny the accuracy or truth of

regime (ray-ZHEEM, ri-JEEM): *n.* a way or form of government; a government in power; a period of rule

reinstatement (ree-in-STATE-ment): *n.* restoration to a previous state or position

reiterate (re-IT-uh-rate): *v.* to say or do again, or again and again

relevant (RELL-uh-vuhnt): *adj.* having important bearing on the matter at hand, especially offering evidence that proves or disproves it

relinquish (ri-LING-kwish): *v.* to leave behind; to retreat from or give up; to stop; to release; to yield

relish (RELL-ish): *v.* to eat or drink with pleasure; to have a pleasing taste; to appreciate

renascence (ri-NASS-ents, ri-NASE-nts): *n.* rebirth; restrengthening

rendering (REN-duhr-ing): *n.* a copy or version

rendezvous (RAHN-di-voo, RAHN-day-voo): *n.* a meeting at a set place and time; the place of the meeting; a popular meeting-place

renown (ri-NOWN): *n.* fame

renunciation (ri-nun-see-AY-shun): *n.* rejection; self-denial

replete (ri-PLETE): *adj.* well fed; filled

repressive (ri-PRESS-ivv): *adj.* acting to put or hold down by force; preventing natural or normal expression, activity, or development

repudiate (ri-PYUDE-ee-ate): *v.* to refuse to accept, acknowledge, pay, or have anything to do with; to reject as untrue or unjust

requisition (rek-wuh-ZISH-uhn): *v.* to ask or demand supplies or other needs, especially in writing

residual (ri-ZIJ-uh-wuhl): *adj.* relating to what remains after the rest is taken away; something left that stays effective for some time

resuscitate (ri-SUHS-uh-tate): *v.* to revive from unconsciousness or apparent death

retaliatory (ri-TAL-yuh-tore-ee): *adj.* revengeful; returning in kind

retinue (RET-n-yu): *n.* group of attendants

retrospective (re-truh-SPECK-tivv): *adj.* based on memory; affecting or about things past

revulsion (ri-VUHL-shun): *n.* withdrawal; sense of complete distaste

rhetoric (RETT-uh-rick): *n.* skill in using language, especially in speaking; spoken communication; insincere or pompous language

rift: *n.* a deep crack; a clear space or interval; a break in a bond of affection

righteously (RY-chuhs-lee): *adv.* justifiably; with a sense of being morally right

roster (RAHS-tuhr): *n.* a list of people; the people listed; an itemized list

rubble: *n.* broken fragments of stone; a group of worthless, broken things

rupture: *n.* a breaking apart; a break; a breach of the peace

sack: *v.* to dismiss, especially without delay

salvo (SAL-voh): *n.* a series of gunshots, either all at once or one after the other; a sudden burst; a salute or tribute

sanction (SANGK-shun): *v.* to make valid or binding, usually with a formal procedure; to give authoritative approval or consent

sanction: *n.* a formal decree; official approval; a plan adopted, usually by several nations, to force a nation to stop violating international law or at least to submit to a legal decision on its lawfulness

savvy (SAV-ee): *adj.* knowledgeable; having practical know-how

scatological (skat-el-ODJ-i-kuhl): *adj.* dealing with obscene matters, especially in literature

scathing (SKAYTHE-ing): *adj.* bitterly harsh

scenario (suh-NARE-ee-oh): *n.* a play or film synopsis or outline; a synopsis of a projected course of action or events

schism (SIZ-uhm, SKIZ-uhm): *n.* separation; a break between people, discord, disharmony

scudding: *adj.* driven swiftly by the wind

scuttle: *v.* to sink or attempt to sink by cutting holes; to wreck

seep: *v.* to flow slowly through small openings

sentient (SEN-chuhnt, SENT-ee-uhnt): *n.* aware, especially to impressions of the senses; sensitive in feeling

seriocomic (sir-ee-oo-KAHM-ick): *adj.* combining the serious and the comic

severance (SEV-uh-ruhntz): *n.* the act or state of being cut or ended

shard: *n.* a small, usually brittle fragment

sheaf: *n.* a bundle

shore up: *v.* to give support to

shortfall: *n.* a failure to come up to a goal or need; the amount of the failure

shrewd: *adj.* clever and aware; given to cleverly tricky ways of dealing

simplistic (sim-PLISS-tick): *adj.* tending to oversimplify or be oversimplified, especially by ignoring complicating factors

simulate (SIM-yuh-late): *v.* to copy outwardly, often in order to deceive; to be a superficial copy

simultaneously (sy-muhl-TAY-nee-us-lee): *adv.* at the same time

skepticism (SKEP-tuh-siz-uhm): *n.* an attitude of doubt or suspended judgment

skewed: *adj.* slanted in one direction or to one side

sleazy (SLEE-zee): *adj.* carelessly or cheaply made; cheap or shoddy

smug: *adj.* very self-satisfied

solace (SAHL-us, SOLE-uhs): *n.* comfort, consolation; source of consolation

sorely: *adv.* painfully; extremely

souped-up: *adj.* increased in power or efficiency

specter (also **spectre**) (SPECK-tuhr): *n.* a ghost; something that haunts the mind

spectrum (SPECK-truhm): *n.* a continuous sequence or range

speculate (SPECK-yuh-late): *v.* to think about something casually and inconclusively; to take a business risk in hope of gain

splat: *n.* a splattering or slapping sound

spoils: *n.* something gained by special effort; public office gained by political winners

spontaneous (spahn-TAY-nee-uss): *adj.* arising from natural feeling or momentary impulse; developing without apparent external influence

spoor (SPOOR, SPORE): *n.* a track or trail, especially that of a wild animal

sporadic (spuh-RAD-ick): *adj.* occurring from time to time

spree: *n.* an unrestrained outburst of activity, a binge

spunky: *adj.* full of spirit

spurious (SPYURE-ee-uss): *adj.* illegitimate; having only outward similarity; forged or of wrongly attributed origin; deceitful

squabble (SKWAB-uhl): *n.* a noisy quarrel, usually over trifles

squat: *v.* to sit low to the ground; to settle on property without right, title, or payment of rent

squat: *adj.* low to the ground; disproportionately low or thick

squib: *n.* a short news item; a funny or satiric short speech or writing

stabilize (STAY-buh-lize): *v.* to become, make or hold steady; to limit in fluctuation; to establish a minimum price for

stagnation (stag-NAY-shun): *n.* quality of being motionless or inactive; act of becoming stale

stampede (stam-PEED): *n.* a wild headlong rush of frightened animals; a mass movement of people on common impulse

stigmatize (STIG-muh-tize): *v.* to mark or brand; to describe or identify as being shameful or contemptible

stolid (STAHL-uhd): *adj.* showing no emotion or sensibility; dull

straggle: *v.* to wander off course; to wander away from others of its kind

strangulated (STRANG-gyuh-late-uhd): *adj.* excessively constricted, to the point of being strangled; violently destroyed

strife: *n.* fight, struggle; angry, often violent conflict; struggle for superiority

stringent (STRIN-juhnt): *adj.* tightly bound; strict or severe, especially about rules or standards; marked by scarce money and restricted credit

stump: *v.* to baffle; to walk heavily and clumsily; to travel making political speeches or supporting a cause

suave (SWAHV): *adj.* smooth in performance or finish; smoothly but often superficially polite and friendly

substantive (SUHB-stuhn-tivv): *adj.* real rather than apparent; essential; permanent; substantial

subversion (suhb-VUHR-zhuhn): *n.* overthrow, especially governmental overthrow by persons working secretly within the country

succumb (suh-KUMM): *v.* to yield to greater force or to very great appeal or desire; to be brought to an end by destructive forces

sunder (SUN-duhr): *v.* to break apart, especially with violence

sway: *n.* a controlling influence; ruling power; the ability to influence or control

swelter (SWELL-tuhr): *v.* to suffer from heat

symposium (sim-POH-zee-um): *n.* a formal meeting at which several specialists give short speeches on a topic or related topics; a collection of opinions on a subject, especially if published in a journal; a discussion

syntax (SIN-tax): *n.* a connected or orderly system for the arrangement of parts; the way in which words are put together to form phrases, clauses, or sentences

tack: *n.* a course or method of action

tangible (TAN-juh-buhl): *adj.* able to be touched; real; capable of being appraised at actual or approximate value

tedious (TEED-ee-us): *adj.* tiresomely dull or long; boring

telling: *adj.* weighty; effective

terminate (TUHR-muh-nate): *v.* to end, to form the end of, to reach an end, to serve as an end to; to discontinue the employment of

theological (thee-oh-LODGE-ih-kuhl): *adj.* relating to religion or religious study

tithe (TYTHE): *n.* a small tax

titillation (titt-uhl-AY-shun): *n.* pleasurable excitation

toxic (TOCK-sick): *adj.* poisonous; affected by a poison

transcend (trants-SEND): *v.* to rise above or go beyond the limits of; to go beyond ordinary limits; to outdo in some way

transgression (trants-GRESH-un): *n.* the act of going beyond set limits, especially in violation of a command, duty, or law

transience (TRANCH-uhnts): *n.* the quality or state of being transitory, of remaining only briefly; the quality or state of affecting something or producing results beyond itself

traumatize (TROW-ma-tize—as in OW of pain—or TRAW-ma-tize): *v.* to cause injury, especially emotional injury, to someone

trepidation (trepp-uh-DAY-shun): *n.* worry; apprehension

trite: *adj.* commonplace; overused

triumvirate (try-UM-vuhr-uht): *n.* a group of three, especially three rulers

troika (TROY-ka): *n.* a Russian vehicle drawn by three horses abreast; a group of three, especially closely related persons or things

trumped-up: *adj.* untruthfully put together

ubiquitous (yu-BICK-wuht-us): *adj.* being everywhere at the same time; constantly encountered

ultimately (UHL-tuh-muht-lee): *adv.* in the end; finally

unadulterated (un-uh-DULL-tuh-ray-tuhd): *adj.* pure, unmixed

unconscionable (un-KON-shun-uh-buhl): *adj.* not guided by conscience, unscrupulous; unreasonable, excessive; shockingly unfair or unjust

unduly (un-DYU-lee): *adv.* excessively

unilateral (yu-nih-LAT-uh-ruhl): *adj.* having only one side; produced on or directed toward one side; one-sided

unmitigated (un-MIT-uh-gate-uhd): *adj.* not lessened; incapable of change or of being changed

unprecedented (un-PRESS-uh-dent-uhd): *adj.* never having happened before; wonderful; extraordinary

unprepossessing (un-pree-po-ZESS-ing): *adj.* unattractive; uninfluential

untempered (un-TEM-puhrd): *adj.* undiluted; unrestrained

urbane (uhr-BANE): *adj.* very polite and smooth in manner

urchin (UHR-chin): *n.* a mischievous child; a child of the streets

utopian (yu-TOE-pee-uhn): *adj.* having or relating to ideal perfection, or a place of such; impossibly ideal; proposing impractically ideal schemes

vacuity (va-KYU-uh-tee): *n.* empty space; state or fact of being empty, idle, or lacking in ideas or intelligence

vehicle (VEE-uh-kuhl): *n.* a carrier or means of carrying; a medium through which something is achieved or displayed

vendetta (ven-DETT-uh): *n.* a long, bitterly hostile feud

veritable (VER-uht-uh-buhl): *adj.* real, authentic (often used to underscore the aptness of a metaphor)

vernal (VUHR-nuhl): *adj.* relating to spring; fresh, new; youthful

viable (VY-uh-buhl): *adj.* able to live or grow, especially as an independent unit; able to work or develop adequately

vicarious (vy-KARE-ee-us): *adj.* substituting for someone or something else; imaginative or sympathetic participation in someone else's experience

vie (vy): *v.* to battle for superiority; to rival

vindicate (VIN-dick-ate): *v.* to avenge, exonerate, justify, or defend

vintage (VIN-tuhj): *adj.* of old, recognized, or lasting interest, importance, or quality

virtually (VUHRCH-uh-wuh-lee): *adv.* almost entirely; for all practical purposes

visceral (VIS-uh-ruhl): *adj.* felt in, or as if in, the guts; instinctive; dealing with crude or elemental emotions

volatile (VAHL-uht-l): *adj.* lighthearted; easily aroused; explosive; changeable; difficult to get or hold permanently

vogue (VOAG): *n.* popularity; period of being in fashion; something in fashion at a particular time

vulpine (VUHL-pine): *adj.* like a fox; tricky, sly

waive (WAVE): *v.* to let go voluntarily; to keep from enforcement; to postpone from consideration

wage: *v.* to engage in or carry on

wan (WAHN): *adj.* sickly, pale; lacking strength; faint

zealous (ZELL-uhss): strongly, even fanatically interested in or devoted to

ANSWERS

1. **For starters:** 1–disavow, 2–disconcert, 3–eclipsed, 4–educe, 5–elicit, 6–escapism, 7–ex cathedra, 8–deter, 9–detritus, 10–insouciance, 11–indiscreet, 12–impose, 13–pervade, 14–perceive, 15–prerequisite, 16–presage, 17–preclude, 18–retrospective, 19–reconstitute, 20–reiterate.

2. **It's all in how:** 1–c, 2–a, 3–a, 4–d, 5–a, 6–c, 7–b, 8–d, 9–b, 10–b, 11–d, 12–b, 13–a, 14–c, 15–a, 16–c, 17–b, 18–c, 19–a, 20–b.

3. **Mystery istory:** 1–m, 2–k, 3–h, 4–o, 5–e, 6–d, 7–c, 8–p, 9–b, 10–a, 11–f, 12–n, 13–1, 14–g, 15–j, 16–i.

4. **Alphabet soup crossword:** *Across:* 1–abate, 3–hodgepodge, 12–defile, 15–furor, 16–circumspection, 19–mammoth, 23–garb, 26–syntax, 29–obliging, 30–phalanx, 31–fete, 32–lax, 33–abated. *Down:* 2–beneficiary, 4–dint, 5–ploy, 6–orgy, 7–quantum, 8–clout, 9–perm, 10–junta, 11–ominous, 13–empirical, 14–urchin, 17–salvo, 18–impotent, 20–troika, 21–klaxon, 22–nurture, 24–zeal, 25–wage, 27–tilt, 28–vie.

5. **End play #1:** 1–avidly, 2–implacably, 3–prohibitively, 4–deftly, 5–unduly, 6–allegedly, 7–imperatively, 8–obliquely, 9–sorely, 10–ostensibly, 11–righteously, 12–ultimately, 13–affably, 14–perversely, 15–appallingly, 16–indiscreetly, 17–formidably, 18–indissolubly, 19–autonomously, 20–culpably. The words that changed meaning are *unduly* and *sorely* (though *sore* was once used to mean *extreme*).

6. **How verbal are you #1:** 1–admonish, 2–assimilate, 3–buoy up, 4–abort, 5–debrief, 6–divert, 7–demean, 8–co-opt, 9–curb, 10–engineer, 11–embargo, 12–evoke, 13–abate, 14–articulate, 15–broach, 16–eclipse, 17–deploy, 18–careen, 19–augur, 20–defile.

7. **First spotlight:** Key word: Panglossian. 1–pseudo, 2–ad lib, 3–nettle, 4–gibe, 5–limbo, 6–oust, 7–savvy, 8–stump, 9–interim, 10–accolade, 11–nostrum.

8. **Distant relatives:** 1: C; a–1, b–2. 2: G; a–2, b–1. 3: E; a–2, b–1. 4: K; a–1, b–2. 5: H; a–2, b–1. 6: L; a–2, b–1. 7: B; a–1, b–2. 8: I; a–2, b–1. 9: A; a–1, b–2. 10: F; a–2, b–1. 11: P; a–2, b–1. 12: D; a–2, b–1. 13: N; a–2, b–1. 14: R; a–2, b–1. 15: J; a–2, b–1. 16: Q; a–2, b–1. 17: M; a–1, b–2. 18: O; a–1, b–2.

9. **Scrambled maxims:** The following sayings appear: #1 and #2: Make hay while the sun shines. The mice will play while the cat's away. #3 and #5: No fool like an old fool. Monkey see monkey do. #4 and #7: A penny saved is a penny earned. A stitch in time saves nine. #6 and #8: Don't cry over spilt milk. The proof is in the pudding.
   Scrambled maxims #1: Maxim: Make hay while the cat's away. 1–matinal, 2–abstraction, 3–kamikaze, 4–ecology, 5–hokum, 6–abyss, 7–yes, 8–waive, 9–hankering, 10–impair, 11–laze, 12–explicit, 13–theological, 14–hustings, 15–epicenter, 16–comply, 17–amalgam, 18–tangible, 19–solace, 20–agonize, 21–wan, 22–afflict, 23–yay.

10. **Ods and ends:** 1–anodyne, 2–condescend, 3–crocodile tears, 4–incendiary, 5–bland, 6–vendetta, 7–meander, 8–podium, 9–portend, 10–grandiose, 11–lodge, 12–fandango, 13–candor, 14–rendezvous, 15–innuendo, 16–doddering, 17–heartland, 18–methodology, 19–transcend, 20–outmoded, 21–moderate, 22–hinterland, 23–rendering, 24–hodgepodge, 25–parody.

11. **Meet the press:** 1–c, 2–b, 3–a, 4–b, 5–d, 6–c, 7–a, 8–a, 9–c, 10–d, 11–b, 12–c, 13–c, 14–a, 15–a, 16–c, 17–a, 18–d, 19–b, 20–d.

12. **Word twins:** 1–bellicose, belligerent; 2–acrid, mordant; 3–bogus, pseudo; 4–approbation, accolade, laud; 5–abate, alleviate; 6–boisterous, raucous, blatant; 7–ingratiating, conciliatory; 8–educe, elicit, evoke; 9–fluctuate, gyrate; 10–gibe, jape; 11–millenium, apocalypse; 12–offensive, foray; 13–prattle, palaver; 14–outmoded, obsolete; 15–elusive, evasive; 16–disclaimer, disavow; 17–peevish, perverse; 18–alleged, purported; 19–traumatize, afflict, anguish; 20–unilateral, activist.

13. **How does it look?** 1–squat, 2–wan, 3–vulpine, 4–transient, 5–skewed, 6–prominent, 7–souped-up, 8–scudded, 9–ocher, 10–mammoth, 11–macabre, 12–myriad, 13–mufti, 14–drab, 15–gross, 16–doddering, 17–bland, 18–burnished, 19–amorphous, 20–bumbles.

14. **It's personal:** 1–a mentor, 2–a predecessor, 3–a pacifist, 4–a mogul, 5–a menial, 6–an envoy, 7–an enigma, 8–an expatriate, 9–an extraterrestrial, 10–a fledgling, 11–a fundamentalist, 12–an entrepreneur, 13–an escapist, 14–a beneficiary, 15–a disciple, 16–an acquisitor, 17–an apotheosis, 18–an aspirant, 19–a centenarian, 20–a derelict, 21–a dissident, 22–an adversary, 23–an avatar, 24–a catalyst, 25–an attaché, 26–a belligerent, 27–a cuckold, 28–a zealot, 29–a protégé, 30–an urchin.

15. **Second spotlight:** Key word: gargantuan. 1–gambit, 2–acuity, 3–relinquish, 4–gyrate, 5–admonition, 6–nurture, 7–tedious, 8–urbane, 9–abstraction, 10–negotiate.

16. **Melodrama matrix:** 1–fandango, 2–fiasco, 3–elusive, 4–apocalypse, 5–harkened, 6–hawkish, 7–hinterlands, 8–liquidate, 9–aborted, 10–moderate, 11–legacy, 12–cataclysmic, 13–paradox, 14–urbane, 15–careen, 16–virtual, 17–phalanx, 18–vulpine, 19–urchin, 20–vie, 21–adversary, 22–formidable, 23–amorphous, 24–articulate, 25–gargantuan, 26–spoils, 27–raucous, 28–exact, 29–cordon off, 30–simultaneous, 21–klaxon, 32–triumvirate, 33–assessed, 34–clout, 35–deploy, 36–gambit, 37–goad, 38–farcical, 39–jape.

17. **Substitutions #1:** 1–c, 2–d, 3–a, 4–a, 5–a, 6–b, 7–c, 8–b, 9–b, 10–c, 11–a, 12–a, 13–d, 14–b, 15–a, 16–b, 17–d, 18–c, 19–b, 20–b.

18. **Focus on idioms:** the two non-idioms, because each is *one* word, not two, are *co-opt* and *seriocomic*. 1–g, 2–e, 3–1, 4–f, 5–b, 6–c, 7–j, 8–a, 9–i, 10–k, 11–h, 12–n, 13–d, 14–m.

19. **Strong roots:** 1–provocative, 2–invocation, 3–founder, 4–profound, 5–litigious, 6–litigation, 7–cohesive, 8–incoherent, 9–pedestrian, 10–stampede, 11–malice, 12–malign, 13–precipitate, 14–precipice, 15–acrid, 16–acrimony, 17–adversary, 18–adversity, 19–circumvent, 20–circumspect.

20. **Pros and cons:** 1–contentious, 2–context, 3–protégé, 4–profound, 5–contrite, 6–prominent, 7–confrontation, 8–laconic, 9–problematic, 10–contretemps, 11–expropriate, 12–conjecture, 13–congenital, 14–proliferate, 15–propensity, 16–approbation, 17–conciliatory, 18–contingency, 19–province, 20–unconscionable, 21–propound, 22–disconcert, 23–prohibitive, 24–rapprochement, 25–consecrate, 26–condescend, 27–convoluted, 28–probe, 29–reconstitute, 30–provocative.

21. **Meet the press #2:** 1–c, 2–d, 3–c, 4–b, 5–b, 6–a, 7–a, 8–c, 9–b, 10–a, 11–d, 12–a, 13–b, 14–d, 15–c, 16–a, 17–b, 18–a, 19–c, 20–b, 21–b, 22–c, 23–c, 24–a, 25–d.

22. **In a word:** 1: N,c; 2: Y,e; 3: N,g; 4: Y,h; 5: Y,f; 6: N,j; 7: Y,b; 8: N,i; 9: Y,d; 10: N,a.

23. **Make-a-word #1:** highlight word: jurisdiction; 1–logjam, 2–jubilant, 3–argot, 4–acquisitor, 5–skewed, 6–facade, 7–fiasco, 8–chronic, 9–abort, 10–liquidation, 11–foment, 12–fragment.

24. **Onion crossword:** *Across:* 1–anathema, 5–urchin, 7–non, 8–laconic, 9–annihilate, 11–anathema, 13–faction, 16–unmitigated, 19–anonymity, 21–envoy, 25–entitlement, 28–latent, 29–utopian. *Down:* 1–analogy, 2–laconic, 3–annexation, 4–anathema, 6–initiative, 10–influx, 12–anodyne, 14–sunder, 15–fervent, 17–indigent, 18–infused, 20–context, 22–enigma, 23–prune, 24–stump, 26–lant, 27–wan.

25. **Hors d'oeuvres:** 1–m, 2–q, 3–e, 4–a, 5–f, 6–b, 7–h, 8–l, 9–o, 10–c, 11–n, 12–d, 13–p, 14–g, 15–s, 16–j, 17–i, 18–r, 19–k.

26. **Double threat:** 1–coincide, 2–degenerates, 3–escalates, 4–escapist, 5–stampede, 6–derisive, 7–vernal, 8–altruist, 9–stigmatize, 10–zealot.

27. **Theater talk:** 1–c, 2–b, 3–b, 4–a, 5–d, 6–b, 7–d, 8–a, 9–d, 10–b.

28. **Substitutions #2:** 1–a, 2–c, 3–b, 4–d, 5–a, 6–a, 7–b, 8–d, 9–b, 10–c, 11–a, 12–a, 13–c, 14–d, 15–a, 16–b, 17–c, 18–a, 19–b, 20–d.

29. **Battle plan:** 1–k, 2–p, 3–d, 4–j, 5–m, 6–f, 7–q, 8–s, 9–a, 10–h, 11–b, 12–n, 13–c, 14–i, 15–t, 16–e, 17–o, 18–r, 19–l, 20–g.

30. **Loaded language:** 1–vintage, 2–vehicle, 3–simultaneously, 4–ratify, 5–resuscitated, 6–retrospective, 7–ubiquitous, 8–scenario, 9–spectrum, 10–inadvertently, 11–exemplify, 12–contretemps, 13–metaphorically, 14–moratorium, 15–marginally, 16–disclaimer, 17–unprecedented, 18–cosmetic, 19–acronym, 20–liquidated.

31. **The animal kingdom:** 1–hawk, 2–broach, 3–stagnation, 4–crocodile tears, 5–assimilate, 6–squabble, 7–grouse, 8–aspirant, 9–cardinal, 10–ramification, 11–fledgling, 12–incur, 13–mammoth, 14–grasp, 15–ferret, 16–assess, 17–fluke, 18–lambaste, 19–scudding, 20–curtail.

32. **How verbal are you #2:** 1–feign, 2–bruit about, 3–assuage, 4–espouse, 5–default, 6–conjecture, 7–exploit, 8–ferret out, 9–elicit, 10–cordon off, 11–curtail, 12–augment, 13–antagonize, 14–exact, 15–exonerate, 16–dissuade, 17–burnish, 18–amalgamate, 19–fare, 20–ad lib.

33. **Third spotlight:** Key word: mercurial. 1–matinal, 2–erratic, 3–raucous, 4–co-opt, 5–untempered, 6–roster, 7–imponderable, 8–acquisitor, 9–lumps.

34. **In-telligence test:** 1–incendiary, 2–incapacitated, 3–incarnation, 4–indigence, 5–incinerate, 6–indissoluble, 7–inadvertent, 8–indiscretion, 9–incur, 10–ingenuity, 11–influx, 12–ineptitude, 13–individualist, 14–instigate, 15–infused, 16–inspired, 17–insatiable, 18–insouciant, 19–inevitable, 20–ingratiating, 21–inequity, 22–initiative, 23–infamy, 24–interminably, 25–intervene, 26–integral, 27–inured, 28–internecine, 29–intrusive, 30–innuendo.

35. **Scrambled maxims #2:** Maxim: The mice will play while the sun shines. 1–tithe, 2–hustings, 3–epochal, 4–martial, 5–immediacy, 6–cornerstone, 7–epiphany, 8–waive, 9–integral, 10–lax, 11–lodge, 12–plethora, 13–lustrous, 14–appalling, 15–year, 16–wage, 17–hankering, 18–inspire, 19–ludicrous, 20–estuary, 21–titillation,

22–hokum, 23–equilibrium, 24–scenario, 25–unmitigated, 26–nettled, 27–shard, 28–hypothetical, 29–ironic, 30–noncommittal, 31–exact, 32–splat.

36. **After-dinner talk:** 1–c, 2–h, 3–g, 4–m, 5–p, 6–q, 7–o, 8–i, 9–n, 10–s, 11–b, 12–k, 13–a, 14–f, 15–j, 16–l, 17–d, 18–r, 19–t, 20–e.

37. **Ad stumper:** 1–c, 2–a, 3–c, 4–a, 5–b, 6–c, 7–b, 8–d, 9–c, 10–d.

38. **Look-alikes:** 1: a–1, b–2; 2: a–2, b–1; 3: a–1, b–2; 4: a–2, b–1; 5: a–1, b–2; 6: a–1, b–2; 7: a–2, b–1; 8: a–2, b–1; 9: a–2, b–1; 10: a–1, b–2; 11: a–2, b–1; 12: a–2, b–1; 13: a–2, b–1; 14: a–1, b–2; 15: a–1, b–2; 16: a–1, b–2; 2: 17: a–1, b–2; 18: a–2, b–1; 19: a–1, b–2; 20: a–2, b–1.

39. **Anty matter:** 1–jubilant, 2–gargantuan, 3–relevant, 4–recant, 5–quantum,. 6–aberrant, 7–exorbitant, 8–penchant, 9–aspirant, 10–flamboyant, 11–irrelevant, 12–ante, 13–poignant, 14–antagonized, 15–adamant, 16–irreverant, 17–blatant, 18–substantive, 19–mordant, 20–exultant.

40. **A family resemblance:** 1: foster; the other words all contain the meaning *to restrict, to cut off.* 2: anodyne; the others all contain the meaning *bitter.* 3: utopian; the others all contain the meaning *false.* 4: spurious; the others all contain the meaning *real.* 5: impotence; the others all contain the meaning *daring.* 6. *ubiquitous;* the others all contain the meaning *a particular place.* 7: vehicle; the others all contain *book* in their meanings; 8: bumbling; the others all mean *ordinary.* 9. fiscal; the others all contain a *number* in their meanings *(cardinal* means *of first importance).* 10: shard: the others all contain *a collection* in their meanings. 11: legacy: the others all contain the idea *money that must be paid.* 12: inured (meaning *accustomed to accept without question);* the others all contain *questioning* in their meanings. 13: miscalculation; the others are all *positive.* (All have to do with investigation.) 14: ecological, which means *relating to the interaction between organisms and their environment;* the others all relate just to *places.* 15: ineffectual; the others all have to do specifically with *skill.* 16: proscribe; the others are all connected with *crime.* 17: mortification; the others are all connected with *burning.* 18: laud; the others all have *legal* in their meanings. 19: panacea; the others all have *prettifying* in their meanings. 20: overt; the others all have *secret* or *hidden* in their meanings.

41. **Meet the press #3:** 1–b, 2–a, 3–c, 4–a, 5–d, 6–a, 7–d, 8–c, 9–b, 10–b, 11–a, 12–c, 13–a, 14–d, 15–b, 16–c, 17–c, 18–b, 19–a, 20–c.

42. **Scrambled maxims #3:** Maxim: No fool monkey do. 1–nurture, 2–ocher, 3–faltering, 4–ostensible, 5–obliquely, 6–lieu, 7–moribund, 8–oligarch, 9–nostrum, 10–kamikaze, 11–exploit, 12–yank, 13–detrimental, 14–overt.

43. **Desultory crossword:** *Across:* 1–bruit about, 5–trite, 8–lax, 10–if, 11–coin, 12–vie; 15–ex cath, 16–blatant, 17–fied, 18–dint, 20–eat, 22–in, 23–cohesive, 27–meander, 29–barn, 30–garb, 33–skepticism, 34–buoy, 37–rim, 39–ate, 40–inured, 41–heartland, 43–gyrate, 46–snow, 47–puerile. *Down:* 1–bumbling, 2–implacably, 3–bilateral, 4–of, 5–toxic, 6–rice, 7–inadvertence, 9–avatar, 11–ce, 13–tatoo, 14–strife, 16–be, 19–logjam, 21–manipulate, 24–hokum, 25–salvo, 26–vehicle, 27–mawkish, 28–deficit, 31–acuity, 32–roomers, 34–brag, 35–curb, 36–red, 38–on, 42–ale, 44–an, 45–to.

44. **Four-letter words:** 1–p, 2–k, 3–f, 4–s, 5–h, 6–l, 7–n, 8–u, 9–q, 10–r, 11–j, 12–y, 13–aa, 14–cc, 15–v, 16–a, 17–o, 18–bb, 19–b, 20–w, 21–g, 22–c, 23–d, 24–t, 25–e, 26–m, 27–dd, 28–x, 29–z, 30–i.

45. **Make-a-word #2:** highlighted word: authenticator; 1–causal, 2–vogue, 3–explicit, 4–hustle, 5–epicenter, 6–incur, 7–rationale, 8–equilibrium, 9–vicarious, 10–epochal, 11–stabilize, 12–hokum, 13–rift.

46. **Small talk:** 1–e, 2–f, 3–m, 4–g, 5–x, 6–p, 7–s, 8–b, 9–c, 10–j, 11–r, 12–a, 13–t, 14–d, 15–o, 16–q, 17–h, 18–i, 19–u, 20–k, 21–v, 22–l, 23–n, 24–w, 25–y.

47. **Common ents:** 1–latent, 2–transient, 3–prudent, 4–sentient, 5–diligent, 6–imminent, 7–intransigent, 8–potent, 9–divergent, 10–fervent, 11–indigent, 12–renascent, 13–inadvertent, 14–impotent, 15–ambivalent, 16–dissident, 17–quiescent, 18–prominent, 19–stringent, 20–incoherent, 21–transcendent, 22–augment, 23–contingent, 24–circumvent, 25–reinstatement.

48. **Meet the press #4:** 1–c, 2–c, 3–a, 4–d, 5–b, 6–b, 7–a, 8–b, 9–c, 10–a, 11–a, 12–c, 13–b, 14–a, 15–a, 16–d, 17–d, 18–c, 19–c, 20–c.

49. **Double trouble:** 1–vendetta, 2–annexation, 3–noncommittal, 4–profess, 5–pullulate, 6–telling, 7–raffish, 8–shortfall, 9–spoor, 10–redress, 11–irrelevant, 12–titillation, 13–unprepossessing, 14–engineer, 15–erratic, 16–collateral, 17–allegory, 18–cull, 19–spree, 20–seep, 21–peevish, 22–harass, 23–squabble, 24–efficacy, 25–attaché, 26–extraterrestrial, 27–alleviate, 28–effectively, 29–prattle, 30–boycott, 31–transgression, 32–nettle, 33–excessively, 34–savvy, 35–scudding, 36–gross, 37–succumb, 38–bellicose, 39–accolade, 40–ferret, 41–fob off, 42–fruitless, 43–scuttle, 44–innocuous, 45–straggle, 46–repressive, 47–assess, 48–gaffe, 49–dissident, 50–dissuade, 51–domineer, 52–garrulousness, 53–rapprochement, 54–immediacy, 55–incorrigible, 56–imminent, 57–ineffectual, 58–innuendo, 59–offensive, 60–Panglossian, 61–dessicate, 62–congenitally, 63–careen, 64–preemptive, 65–puffery, 66–preoccupied, 67–predecessor, 68–appreciable, 69–assuage, 70–belligerent, 71–colloquial, 72–ground swell, 73–virtually, 74–fecklessness, 75–millennium, 76–officious, 77–irreverent, 78–doddering, 79–interrogate, 80–impeccable, 81–indissoluble, 82–approbation, 83–annihilate, 84–attributable, 85–differentiate.

50. **Scrambled maxims #4:** Maxim: A penny saved saves nine. 1–abyss, 2–problematic, 3–enigma, 4–spectrum, 5–ambivalence, 6–vicarious, 7–empirical, 8–demeanor, 9–strangulated, 10–affable, 11–vindicate, 12–entitlement, 13–suave, 14–indiscreet, 15–equilibrium.

51. **Fourth spotlight:** Key word: blitzkrieg. 1–beneficiary, 2–lambaste, 3–integral, 4–traumatize, 5–zealous, 6–klaxon, 7–rationale, 8–intervene, 9–evoke, 10–gambit.

52. **Substitutions #3:** 1–a, 2–c, 3–d, 4–c, 5–a, 6–b, 7–a, 8–a, 9–b, 10–c, 11–b, 12–b, 13–d, 14–c, 15–d, 16–a, 17–d, 18–c, 19–a, 20–b.

53. **True or false:** 1–h, 2–g, 3–q, 4–f, 5–n, 6–p, 7–r, 8–e, 9–a, 10–y, 11–s, 12–b, 13–t, 14–j, 15–c, 16–v, 17–1, 18–d, 19–u, 20–i, 21–w, 22–m, 23–k, 24–o, 25–x.

54. **More family resemblances:** 1: innocuous; the other words all contain the meaning *harm*. 2: vintage; the others all contain the meaning

youth. 3: anonymity; the others all contain the idea of *naming.*
4: empirical, which is based on *evidence;* the others all contain the idea
without evidence. 5: institute; the others all contain the meaning *stop.*
6: salvo; the others contain the meaning *destruction.* 7: fiscal; the
others contain the meaning *lack of money.* 8: boycott; the others are
all *active.* 9: minuscule, the others all show *excess.* 10: incorrigible; the
others all contain the meaning *helpful.* 11: putative; the others all have
to do with *death.* 12: derisive; the others all contain the idea of
silliness. 13: stolid; the others all show *emotion.* 14: menial; the others
are all *bigwigs.* 15: junta; the others are all *individuals.* 16: skeptic;
the others all *believe* in something. 17: palaver; the others all suggest
one speaker. 18: cuckold; the others all contain the meaning *trickery.*
(A cuckold may or may not have been tricked.) 19: lax; the others all
contain the meaning *careful.* 20: dissident; the others all contain the
meaning *a follower.*

55. Shades of meaning: 1: a–2, b–1; 2: a–2, b–1; 3: a–1, b–2; 4: a–2, b–1;
5: a–1, b–2; 6: a–1, b–2; 7: a–2, b–1; 8: a–1, b–2; 9: a–1, b–2;
10: a–2, b–1; 11: a–1, b–2; 12: a–2, b–1; 13: a–2, b–1;
14: a–1, b–2; 15: a–2, b–1; 16: a–1, b–2; 17: a–2, b–1; 18: a–1, b–2;
19: a–2, b–1; 20: a–2, b–1.

56. Meet the press #5: 1–c, 2–b, 3–a, 4–b, 5–a, 6–c, 7–a, 8–a, 9–d, 10–b,
11–c, 12–b, 13–c, 14–a, 15–d, 16–b, 17–a, 18–a, 19–c, 20–c.

57. Scrambled maxims #5: Maxim: Monkey see like an old fool.
1–metaphor, 2–overt, 3–nostrum, 4–kamikaze, 5–explicit, 6–you,
7–squib, 8–empirical, 9–estuary, 10–lustrous, 11–innocuous, 12–klaxon,
13–ecological, 14–argot, 15–negotiate, 16–oust, 17–ludicrous, 18–deft,
19–furor, 20–offensive, 21–obstructionist, 22–lumps.

58. Personalities: 1–f, 2–j, 3–n, 4–c, 5–1, 6–i, 7–a, 8–q, 9–e, 10–t, 11–b,
12–m, 13–k, 14–o, 15–g, 16–s, 17–r, 18–d, 19–p, 20–h.

59. No matter: 1–anodyne, 2–innocuous, 3–monologist, 4–anonymous,
5–demeanor, 6–noncommittal, 7–autonomous, 8–anomaly, 9–renowned,
10–nostrum.

60. How verbal are you #3: 1–deter, 2–convolute, 3–falter, 4–educe,
5–disavow, 6–infuse, 7–hamper, 8–jest, 9–meander, 10–intervene,
11–incur, 12–founder, 13–fathom, 14–condescend, 15–inspire, 16–goad,
17–consecrate, 18–malign, 19–escalate, 20–mimic.

61. A nation of ations: 1–lamentation, 2–fluctuation, 3–polarization,
4–trepidation, 5–confrontation, 6–invocation, 7–litigation, 8–stagnation,
9–approbation, 10–renunciation, 11–liquidation, 12–formulation,
13–aberration, 14–titillation, 15–mortification, 16–ramification,
17–adulation, 18–denunciation, 19–incarnation, 20–annexation.

62. Current events: 1–b, 2–b, 3–b, 4–a, 5–a, 6–c, 7–d, 8–b, 9–a, 10–d,
11–c, 12–a, 13–d, 14–b, 15–c, 16–c, 17–a, 18–d, 19–d, 20–d.

63. Shades of meaning #2: 1: a–2, b–1; 2: a–1, b–2; 3: a–1, b–2; 4: a–2,
b–1; 5: a–2, b–1; 6: a–1, b–2; 7: a–2, b–1; 8: a–2, b–1; 9: a–1, b–2;
10: a–2, b–1; 11: a–2, b–1; 12: a–1, b–2; 13: a–1, b–2; 14: a–1, b–2;
15: a–2, b–1; 16: a–1, b–2; 17: a–2, b–1; 18: a–1, b–2; 19: a–1, b–2;
20: a–2, b–1.

64. **Some more personalities:** 1–r, 2–g, 3–i, 4–a, 5–l, 6–m, 7–c, 8–q, 9–o, 10–d, 11–h, 12–s, 13–f, 14–b, 15–k, 16–j, 17–e, 18–p, 19–t, 20–n.

65. **Euphemisms:** 1–t, 2–c, 3–k, 4–b, 5–w, 6–r, 7–y, 8–g, 9–a, 10–q, 11–m, 12–f, 13–1, 14–d, 15–u, 16–j, 17–h, 18–e, 19–x, 20–v, 21–p, 22–i, 23–n, 24–s, 25–o.

66. **Make-a-word #3:** highlighted word: unprepossessing; 1–quiescent, 2–unduly, 3–rupture, 4–visceral, 5–entity, 6–purported, 7–volatile, 8–schism, 9–salvo, 10–replete, 11–roster, 12–sorely, 13–viable, 14–revulsion, 15–degenerate.

67. **X marks the spot crossword:** *Across:* 1–extraterrestrial, 2–polate, 3–paradox, 5–exult, 6–exonerate, 8–over, 9–extension, 13–influx, 14–lax, 16–toxic, 17–context, 18–exemplify, 19–phalanx, 20–paradox. *Down:* 1–expropriate, 4–over, 5–exemplify, 7–annexation, 10–exact, 11–klaxon, 12–syntax, 15–toxic.

68. **Meet the press #6:** 1–d, 2–a, 3–b, 4–b, 5–a, 6–d, 7–a, 8–c, 9–b, 10–a, 11–a, 12–d, 13–b, 14–a, 15–c, 16–c, 17–a, 18–a, 19–b, 20–c.

69. **Scrambled maxims #6:** Maxim: Don't cry in the pudding. 1–defile, 2–obliquely, 3–noncommittal, 4–troika, 5–chestnut, 6–relevant, 7–impeccable, 8–transience, 9–hamper, 10–ecology, 11–primer, 12–unprecedented, 13–detente, 14–disciple, 15–immediacy, 16–nettle, 17–grievance.

70. **It's about time:** 1–i, 2–g, 3–d, 4–f, 5–h, 6–c, 7–a, 8–b, 9–j, 10–e, 11–r, 12–o, 13–m, 14–p, 15–k, 16–1, 17–s, 18–q, 19–t, 20–n.

71. **Family resemblances #3:** 1: altruistic; the others all contain the meaning *starting trouble.* 2: lambaste; the others all contain the idea of *peacemaking.* 3: raffish; the others all contain the idea of *sophistication.* 4: euphemism; the others all contain the meaning *vulgar.* 5: facade; the others all contain the meaning *intuitive understanding.* 6: shrewd; the others all contain the meaning *insistence.* 7: troika; the others all contain the meaning *rule.* 8: intrusive; the others all contain the idea of *division.* 9: pullulate; the others all contain the idea of *the actual number is unknown.* 10: burnished; all others are *dull* in appearance. 11: disparity; all others contain the meaning *not genuine.* 12: hypothetical; all others contain the meaning *truth.* 13: perfunctory; all others contain the meaning *not performing well.* 14: protégé; all others contain the meaning *group of people.* 15: trepidation (which means *worry);* all others contain the meaning *to wonder about.* 16: prerequisite; all others contain the meaning *of future time.* 17: apathetic; all others contain the meaning *strong* (strong wish, strong liking, strong inclination). 18: cardinal; all others contain the meaning *lack of measurability.* 19: perspective; all others contain the meaning *picture or copy.* 20: cull; all others contain the idea of *discomfort.*

72. **Why y? why not?:** 1–incendiary, 2–methodology, 3–jockey, 4–immediacy, 5–epiphany, 6–desultory, 7–parody, 8–orgy, 9–chicanery, 10–anomaly, 11–arbitrary, 12–ratify, 13–retaliatory, 14–apathy, 15–centenary, 16–efficacy, 17–sleazy, 18–spunky, 19–estuary, 20–vacuity.

73. **How verbal are you #4:** We list the verbs in infinitive form: 1–nurture, 2–hustle, 3–jockey, 4–shore up, 5–impair, 6–permeate,

7–proscribe, 8–stampede, 9–sack, 10–obliterate, 11–presage, 12–swelter, 13–ponder, 14–hanker, 15–lament, 16–subvert, 17–stabilize, 18–propound, 19–probe, 20–pilfer.

74. **Cat's play:** 1–scatological, 2–ex cathedra, 3–dessicated, 4–authenticator, 5–bifurcates, 6–invocation, 7–provocative, 8–scathing, 9–catalytic, 10–vindicated.

75. **Substitutions #4:** 1–b, 2–c, 3–d, 4–a, 5–b, 6–a, 7–b, 8–d, 9–a, 10–b, 11–b, 12–c, 13–a, 14–c, 15–a, 16–d, 17–b, 18–a, 19–c, 20–c.

76. **Double threat #2:** 1–jape, 2–pedestrian, 3–anguish, 4–sheaf, 5–aftermath, 6–theologian, 7–anomalies, 8–espouse, 9–sentience, 10–centenary.

77. **O-o crossword:** *Across:* 1–analogous, 6–unconscionable, 12–loot, 14–do, 15–outmoded, 16–hodgepodge, 18–foil, 19–tool, 20–boo, 21–ominous, 22–you, 24–convoluted, 26–ecological, 29–co-opt, 31–lob, 32–contentious, 35–SRO, 37–sort, 38–it, 39–zoo, 40–trio, 41–SOS, 43–of, 46–soap, 48–toss, 50–over, 51–fools, 52–polarize, 53–foot, 54–fluke, 58–moratorium, 61–go, 62–propound, 63–limbo, 64–moo. *Down:* 1–apotheosis, 2–autonomous, 4–oleo, 5–so, 7–nod, 8–spontaneous, 9–odes, 10–no, 11–buoy, 13–theological, 17–goo, 23–holocaust, 25–boisterous, 27–cordon off, 28–goof, 30–poor, 33–toot, 34–stolid, 36–mufti, 42–coo, 44–too, 45–sloop, 46–spoor, 47–pa, 49–Oz, 55–Leo, 56–ego, 58–MP, 59–to, 60–id.

78. **Scrambled maxims #7:** Maxim: A stitch in time is a penny earned. 1–amalgam, 2–scathing, 3–tedious, 4–insouciance, 5–tack, 6–cosmetic, 7–hankering, 8–inspire, 9–triumvirate, 10–imposition, 11–magnific, 12–envoy, 13–integrate, 14–squatter, 15–apathy, 16–province, 17–epochal, 18–eventuality, 19–arbitrary, 20–rift, 21–epicenter, 22–detente.

79. **Look-alikes #2:** 1: a–1, b–2; 2: a–1, b–2; 3: a–2, b–1; 4: a–2, b–1; 5: a–1, b–2; 6: a–2, b–1; 7: a–1, b–2; 8: a–2, b–1; 9: a–1, b–2; 10: a–1, b–2; 11: a–1, b–2; 12: a–2, b–1; 13: a–2, b–1; 14: a–1, b–2; 15: a–2, b–1; 16: a–2, b–1; 17: a–1, b–2; 18: a–2, b–1; 19: a–2, b–1; 20: a–2, b–1, c–3.

80. **Fifth spotlight:** highlight word: sanctioned. 1–adversity, 2–apathy, 3–epiphany, 4–muck, 5–ostensibly, 6–epicenter, 7–audacious, 8–entity, 9–laze, 10–unduly.

81. **Happenings:** 1–j, 2–b, 3–l, 4–k, 5–a, 6–o, 7–c, 8–m, 9–d, 10–p, 11–n, 12–e, 13–t, 14–q, 15–f, 16–s, 17–r, 18–g, 19–x, 20–u, 21–h, 22–y, 23–i, 24–w, 25–v.

82. **Back problems:** 1–recant, 2–reinstate, 3–reconstitute, 4–refute, 5–revulsion, 6–renunciation, 7–renascence, 8–reiterate, 9–relinquish, 10–retrospective, 11–residual, 12–requisition, 13–resuscitate, 14–redress, 15–retaliatory, 16–renown, 17–repressive, 18–repudiate.

83. **Word twins #2:** 1–latency, propensity; 2–languor, impotence; 3–deter, hamper; 4–eclipsed, obliterated; 5–tithe, levy; 6–disclaimer, repudiation; 7–dilatory, desultory; 8–hustle, jockey; 9–contentious, divisive; 10–animosity, acrimony; 11–renunciate, repudiate; 12–avatar, incarnation; 13–prohibit, preclude; 14–vintage, obsolete; 15–divergent, divisive; 16–parochial, marginal; 17–exploit, manipulate; 18–chagrined, disconcerted, mortified; 19–unprecedented, epochal; 20–amalgam, hodgepodge.

148

84. **Word work-out:** 1–j, 2–c, 3–k, 4–hh, 5–g, 6–a, 7–d, 8–h, 9–e, 10–f, 11–i, 12–l, 13–s, 14–m, 15–q, 16–r, 17–n, 18–t, 19–u, 20–x, 21–v, 22–o, 23–aa, 24–cc, 25–w, 26–p, 27–z, 28–bb, 29–dd, 30–gg, 31–ff, 32–ii, 33–b, 34–y, 35–ee.

85. **4-D crossword:** 1e–sack, 1s–scuttle, 2e–scathing, 2se–spree, 2s–stolid, 2sw–squat, 3e–smug, 3se–spla, 3s–spoor, 3sw–sway, 4e–ent, 5e–stabilize, 5se–stig, 5s–straggle, 6e–symposia, 6se–scenario, 6sw–spoils, 7e–specter, 7se–sleazy, 7s–soup up, 8s–ske, 8sw–syntax, 9s–suave, 9sw–sleazy, 10e–sol, 10s–simplis, 10se–sunder, 10sw–shrewd, 11e–sap, 11s–sack, 11sw–seep, 12e–spunky, 13e–seriocomic.

86. **Scrambled maxims #8:** Maxim: The proof is spilt milk. 1–transcend, 2–harangue, 3–expropriate, 4–preoccupied, 5–regime, 6–ocher, 7–officious, 8–facade, 9–inured, 10–subversive, 11–symposium, 12–professed, 13–innuendo, 14–lodge, 15–tangible, 16–mount, 17–interrogation.

87. **Meet the press #7:** 1–c, 2–b, 3–d, 4–a, 5–b, 6–a, 7–c, 8–a, 9–c, 10–d, 11–b, 12–c, 13–d, 14–a, 15–a, 16–c, 17–d, 18–a, 19–b, 20–b.

88. **Words of one syllable:** 1–jape, 2–lax, 3–broach, 4–bland, 5–clout, 6–feign, 7–fluke, 8–grasp, 9–goad, 10–probed, 11–lodge, 12–lumps, 13–squib, 14–spoils, 15–stump, 16–tack, 17–spoor, 18–splat, 19–sheaf, 20–shrewd, 21–prune, 22–vogue, 23–vie, 24–waive, 25–waged.

89. **Sixth spotlight:** spotlight word: debrief. 1–sporadic, 2–vernal, 3–equilibrium, 4–lustrous, 5–bristle, 6–bolster, 7–aftermath.

90. **Some more euphemisms:** 1–x, 2–w, 3–y, 4–n, 5–m, 6–c, 7–v, 8–b, 9–a, 10–e, 11–o, 12–j, 13–g, 14–p, 15–i, 16–h, 17–k, 18–l, 19–f, 20–d, 21–s, 22–r, 23–u, 24–q, 25–t.

91. **Double-takes crossword:** *Across:* 1–assimilate, 4–profess, 7–spoor, 8–Panglossian, 12–puffery, 14–too, 15–spree, 16–vie, 17–engineer, 20–virtually, 21–collateral, 22–indiscreet, 23–mammoth, 24–ass, 26–wan, 27–ill, 28–shortfall, 30–peevish, 31–ground swell, 32–excessive, 36–succumb, 37–off, 41–tee, 42–soot, 45–assuage, 47–unprepossessing, 48–transgression, 49–small. *Down:* 1–appreciable, 2–sin, 3–trio, 4–pi(x), 6–on, 9–grill, 10–steel, 11–sorry, 13–fruitless, 18–no, 19–gloss, 25–boss, 26–wage, 29–hee, 33–co-opt, 34–so, 35–if, 37–mogul, 38–bee, 40–tree, 41–toss, 42–sum, 43–on, 44–ass, 46–SOS.

92. **How verbal are you #5:** 1–incinerating, 2–perceive, 3–refuted, 4–pervaded, 5–rendezvous, 6–moderated, 7–relish, 8–precludes, 9–terminate, 10–repudiated, 11–ruptured, 12–relinquish, 13–transgress, 14–resuscitated, 15–sundered, 16–requisition, 17–foster, 18–inured, 19–reiterated, 20–hampers.

93. **It's personal #2:** 1–degenerate, 2–augur, 3–euphoric, 4–activist, 5–incarnation, 6–specter, 7–paradigm, 8–impotent, 9–altruist, 10–theologian, 11–ambivalent, 12–utopian, 13–autonomous, 14–populist, 15–inspiration, 16–pragmatist, 17–intervenor, 18–monologist, 19–jester, 20–oligarch.

94. **Words, words, words:** 1–acronym, 2–allegory, 3–context, 4–colloquial, 5–syntax, 6–trite, 7–squabble, 8–squib, 9–articulation, 10–euphemisms, 11–formulation, 12–banal, 13–harangue, 14–grouse, 15–garrulous, 16–incoherent, 17–innuendo, 18–metaphor, 19–lamentations, 20–mimicry.

95. **End play #2:** 1–false, 2–true, 3–false, 4–false, 5–false, 6–true, 7–true, 8–false, 9–true, 10–false, 11–false, 12–true, 13–false, 14–false, 15–true, 16–false, 17–false, 18–true, 19–true, 20–false.
96. **Loaded words #2:** 1–pragmatist, 2–differentiate, 3–abyss, 4–agonize, 5–vicariously, 6–prerequisite, 7–bristled, 8–chestnut, 9–retinue, 10–limbo, 11–coincide, 12–perspective, 13–purge, 14–holocaust, 15–fundamentalist, 16–debriefed, 17–requisition, 18–quiescent, 19–apocalyptic, 20-momentum.